BEADWORK

To Cinzia Embrioni

Thanks to my friends Anna Maria Meriggi, Simona Risi, Caterina Magrotti, Nadia Ghisolfi, Carla Lobianco.
To my teacher Giovanna Marchesi Poggi.
To Andrea Boccardi for his help in the floreal compositions.
To Cristina Sperandeo.
To the photographer Alberto Bertoldi and to editorial staff.
Special thanks to Renata and Giorgia from "La Perla Veneziana", Murano, Italy, for historical research, the miniature of the furnace, and the oil lamp beads.

Metric Conversion Chart

To convert	to	multiply by
Inches	Centimeters	2.54
Centimeters	Inches	0.4
Feet	Centimeters	30.5
Centimeters	Feet	0.03
Yards	Meters	0.9
Meters	Yards	1.1
Sq. Inches	Sq. Centimeters	6.45
Sq. Centimeters	Sq. Inches	0.16
Sq. Feet	Sq. Meters	0.09
Sq. Meters	Sq. Feet	10.8
Sq. Yards	Sq. Meters	0.8
Sq. Meters	Sq. Yards	1.2
Pounds	Kilograms	0.45
Kilograms	Pounds	2.2
Ounces	Grams	28.4
Grams	Ounces	0.04

Editorial direction: Cristina Sperandeo
Photography: Alberto Bertoldi
Graphic design: Paola Masera and Amelia Verga with Beatrice Brancaccio
Layout: Annamaria Cerri
Cover: Damiano Viscardi
Translation: Studio Queens

Donatella Ciotti

BEADWORK

NORTH LIGHT BOOKS
Cincinnati, Ohio

TABLE OF CONTENTS

INTRODUCTION

Beads are back. They are back in purple irises, in May roses, in pink morning glories that climb summer hedges, in red poppies and blue cornflowers that stain wheat fields, in opulent sunflowers.

They make arabesques creating small plants that will bring each season's colors and perfumes into our homes. Illuminating necklines and sparkling with every movement of a hand, they are mounted in refined jewelry that not even diamonds, rubies and sapphires can put to shame.

Born of a revived interest in beadwork, this book shows how to create handmade objects of rare beauty with little difficulty through detailed, step-by-step, illustrated instructions.

A HISTORY

Beads, whether made with semi-precious stones, with glass, or from animal bones and teeth, have aroused great interest and fascination in various civilizations, from prehistoric times to the present. The first forms of beadmaking for commerce appeared around 6000 B.C. in the Middle East, where they were considered amulets.

Whatever the exact circumstances of glass's invention, the trading of Phoenicia's siliceous sands and Egypt's natron (a mineral composed of sodium and aluminum destined to be employed as a fusing substance in glassmaking) was certainly fundamental.

The Phoenicians had a large influence on the diffusion of glass and, therefore, of glass beads, in which they traded throughout the Mediterranean. Phoenician beads were produced by dripping a vitreous paste of various colors into the center of bones or stones, and they were usually destined to adorn the bodies and robes of the dead and to accompany them into the netherworld as propicious offerings.

In Mesopotamia, on the other hand, beads lost

"Evening gown" dress for grandmother's quill. This splendid workmanship executed like "lace-work" with needle and thread, counting each single bead, is nowadays used to make collars for exclusive clothes and lady's evening handbags.

their significance as amulets and became symbols of wealth and social status.

The Egyptians produced beads by dripping a vitreous paste, commonly blue, green or black, onto fragments of quartz. Thereby, the beads, called *Faience*, became even more precious and, when mounted in pure gold, were worn by the Pharaohs, again as amulets.

Between the third and second centuries B.C., Greece stood out for the variety of forms and the vivacious colors of the beads it produced. The island of Rhodes may have been an important center of bead production.

In the Hellenistic period, Alexandria became the most active bead production center due to a new technique called "glass mosaic" (400 B.C.) in which variously colored tubes of both hollow and solid glass were utilized.

The Romans, through the use of "glassmakers' soap" (manganese dioxide) eliminated the colored impurities from glass. They could, therefore, produce small bars of glass for mosaics, milk-glass, cameos and decorations. With the discovery of the glassblower's pipe, they began large scale production of glass containers for domestic use. The Roman beads, produced until A.D. 400 within the empire, were highly valued for an artistic level of workmanship and range of color equalled only by later Venetian productions.

In ancient times, along with Egypt and Rome, Islam was also a center for glass production and, consequently, for beads, which were considered talismans. New techniques were developed to produce the famous "eye", "folded", "festoon", and "feather" beads.

Small frames for holy pictures often to be seen on night tables toward the beginning of the last century. The high quality workmanship of the braid is still very fashionable today.

After the fall of Damascus, in 1401, glass production in the Islamic world began to decline with only sporadic residual centers of craftsmanship in Asia Minor. Venice then became the most important center of glass and glass bead production, using all of the techniques from centuries past.

The first documents bearing witness to glassmaking in Venice go back to the tenth century with the production of bottles for domestic use. Throughout the thirteenth century the number of workshops grew, some starting specifically for the production of beads. Given the development of this art, the Venetian glassmakers joined together in a trade association named "Scuola" or "School".

Toward the end of the thirteenth century the art of the "*perleri*" (beadworkers) was such a developed activity in the city of Venice that, in 1284, the trade corporation called "*Mariegola dei Cristalleri*" established regulations to ensure against the substitution of glass beads, the famous Paternoster beads, for rosary beads made of rock crystals.

By decree of the city council in 1291 all the glassmaking furnaces, except the small workshops which produced the Paternosters and semi-precious stones, had to move to the island of Murano and promise to keep secret the glassmaking techniques.

Beads were commonly used to create rosaries and to imitate precious stones—in 1445 it was so hard to recognize rock crystals from the imitations that the Senate of Venice was forced to make a decree that inflicted severe punishments both on the makers and the dealers of false stones.

Around 1475 new methods of bead making were born, beginning with a hollow tube cut into many small pieces and then chiseled into various rounded shapes, producing many new categories of Paternosters.

Thus, the new trade of the "*margheriteri*" was born, which in 1604, merged into a single corporation with the "Cristalleri", giving birth to a larger corporation that included all of the arts of bead manufacturing concentrated in the School of San Francesco della Vigna and their Patron Saint Antonio Abate. Around the sixteenth century a new type of workmanship appeared called "*a lume*" or "*a lucerna*" (oil lamp). Like the other types, it is impossible to know who invented "oil lamp" beads; one can only hypothesize that they represented an evolution in the Paternosters, since they also were dripped onto an iron

Evening bag from the end of the nineteenth century was made from tulle and embroidered with tiny blue and white beads in a delicate, Greek pattern. The bottom is gathered and completed with a lovely tassel.

The many nuances of this refined flower are obtained by a weaving technique using a rigid base onto which veins of variegated beads are connected.

wire, but in this case, a solid tube was used instead of the hollow one used to make the paternosters, and they were worked over the fire of an oil lamp.

This new method allowed such startling innovations in the Venetian beads' colors, dimensions and shapes that the beads became famous and valued throughout the known world.

Between the seventeenth and eighteenth centuries the beadmakers had developed a special technique using various materials – probably wax, silver, salt and fish scales – to produce beads that imitated those famous in Islam.

In 1606, in Venice alone, there were 251 glass bead workshops, though this number was destined to shrink down to 22 in 1764 and, because of the war between France and Austria, down to only 12 in 1836.

Only after the end of the war did the glass and bead industry regain new vigor. By the early 1800s, production of the "*conterie*" or seed beads, used for making fringes, buttons, buckles, on both clothing and upholstery (pillow) fabrics, had reached a nearly industrial level. In the period between 1867 and 1874, there was a large demand for the so-called "*mac*" beads (black faceted beads) by French artisans. The demand dried up in 1888 after the commercial treaty with France had lapsed. However, in 1920 demand increased again with the influence of great ateliers whose revolutionary designs in feminine fashions led to a rise in exports.

In 1898 on the island of Murano, where practically all of the Venetian glass workmanship had moved, there were three large manufacturers of seed beads with 443 male and 268 female workers. This is not counting the truly historical figures called the "*impiraresse*" (though few exist today), who in great numbers worked at home. The job of the latter women consisted in stringing tiny seed beads, which they held in a bowl on their knees, onto special cotton threads ("*asse*"), using very long, thin needles grouped into combs. Between the late 1800s and the early 1900s, glass beads had found admirers among the masters of Art Nouveau, such as Emile Gall, the great glass artist. A few years later, they are found in the productions of Tiffany and, in the 1920s, they triumphed in the refined feminine fashions of the day. Bead trade has not had a slow-down during the past century, even though generally used only in certain sectors of the marketplace.

Recently there has been a revival of interest in beadwork as a hobby and a growing number of people with ability and skill, good taste and enthusiasm are discovering the pleasure of creating real works of art with beads.

Venetian "conterie" (seed beads) from the beginning of the twentieth century are used in these two splendid flowers made with the post technique.

"HISTORICAL" BEADS

THE "CONTERIE" OR SEED BEADS

The word "*conteria*" (seed beads) could have its origins in the ancient *contigia*, which means "ornament," in which case it would refer to the use of beads as jewelry. Otherwise, it could come from "*contarelcontante*" (to count), which would be a reference to the use of beads as money by certain groups of people.

The "*conteria*" beads are obtained by working with hollow tubes of glass in special furnaces. The entire cycle of the glassmaking process is entrusted to a group of workers composed of a master, two assistants, a puller and the "*conzaor*" who prepares the mix of minerals which, when fused, form the glass. The assistant extracts from the melting pot a certain quantity of melted glass with a 1.6m (5') long iron rod and, with the use of a tool called the "brass," obtains a cylinder. Then, after having heated the cylinder to the correct temperature, the master makes a hole in the center with an iron instrument, fixing a rod of iron called the *conzaura* on one end and the glassblower's pipe on the other end. Through the combined action of the glassblower and the puller, so called because he pulls the conzaura from the opposite end, a tube of the desired size is obtained. After it is cooled, the tube is cut to 1m (3') in length. From the hollow tube of small diameter, many small cylinders are produced through a cutting process.

The last phase in the seed bead process consists of rubbing the small cylinders with a mixture of lime and coal to prevent their holes from clogging, after which they are put in the furnace again. In the furnace, they are kept in continual movement to transform the cylinders into spheres which, after cooling, are cleaned. Beads are then sorted according to their diameters and, finally, are cleaned and shined with sand and bran.

This miniature shows an oil lamp bead furnace from the period around 1930. In the corner is the oven used for preparing the glass paste from which one obtained the solid glass tube, which produced the oil lamp beads. In the middle, women working the beads. Venice, private collection "La Perla Veneziana".

THE "OIL-LAMP" BEADS

Piles of old beads called "powder beads" because of their tiny holes. Today they are no longer produced because the very small needles needed to thread these beads are no longer available. Venice, private collection "La Perla Veneziana".

The production of the oil lamp beads was perfected around the sixteenth century. They got their name from the oil lamps used to drip the glass around an iron wire covered by a refractory substance. Its flame, fueled by animal fat or oil, was maintained by using a bellows. With this type of workmanship, unchanged through the centuries, beadmakers with artistic abilities began to create uniquely colored beads, sometimes blending different colors together, using floral decorations, inserting tiny, semi-precious stones as well as other decorative elements.

The beadmaker has all around him, on shelves and near at hand, copper wire, glassblowing tubes of various sizes and colors, pliers, "ends" (extremely thin sticks of colored glass or filigree), powdered or filigreed aventurine, bunches of gold and silver leaf. On his work counter, a blow torch and an air compressor push the flame (800–1000°C, 1472–1832°F) horizontally toward a fireproof stone burner in front of it. The artisan, protected by a window, heats the glass rod, which he holds in his gloved right hand while in the other he holds a copper wire onto which the glass will drip in the desired quantity.

This is the way most solid-colored beads (called *schiette*) are produced. But a master beadmaker can create beads of more than one color by preparing a base (*anima*) in opaque glass and covering it with transparent glass, or by using filigrees as paintbrushes, creating flowered beads. The shape is created while the glass is still hot by using pliers or bronze molds. Once finished, the bed is immersed in ashes to cool slowly, thus avoiding breaks and cracks. When cooling is completed, the copper wire is eliminated and the hole remains intact. Although contemporary glassmakers work in modern laboratories, they use techniques as old as the profession itself.

This small lady's bag, which goes back to the year 1890, shows a jacquard design carried out with knitting needles. The beads were threaded to create single strings, following a chosen design, counting all beads in order to have the least possible number of joints. Time has left no mark on this creation, which, over these long years, presents itself fully intact in all its beauty.

GETTING
STARTED

COMMON TYPES OF BEADS

SOLID-COLORED, OPAQUE "SCHIETTE" BEADS
These solid-colored beads can imitate gemstones such as jade, coral and turquoise. Using aventurine powder or other minerals you can obtain imitations of lapis lazuli and amber.

SUBMERGED BEADS
These beads are obtained by dripping fused glass onto a copper wire. They have a center of pastel glass and/or fragments of aventurine or colored cylinders, all of which is covered by a layer of transparent glass.

MOSAIC BEADS
These beads are obtained by dripping a core of pastel glass (usually blue). By using special tweezers the tiny *murrina* cylinders are placed next to each other onto the core. Everything is then amalgamated through a heating process and placed into a bronze mold to create the desired shape. A final heating makes the surface perfectly smooth.

FLOWERED BEADS
The production of these beads begins with the preparation of the ends (thin sticks of colored glass) in filigree, in colored pastel cylinders, in aventurine, and of the flat ends, also in aventurine.
After having dripped the correct quantity of glass on the copper wire, the beadmaker gives it a spherical shape (although other shapes are possible). Using a flat aventurine end he divides the bead into two hemispheres.
At this point, with the thin aventurine end, he decorates each hemisphere with a swag. Now the stars of the creation become the ends or filigree ends, used by the beadmaker like paintbrushes to make rosebud designs as well as other kinds of flowers with blue and yellow dots.
This is how the classic flowered bead is produced, but master beadmakers continually work with new designs and colors. Their creative genius enables them to produce tiny masterpieces using different filigrees, silver and gold leaf, and rare colors.

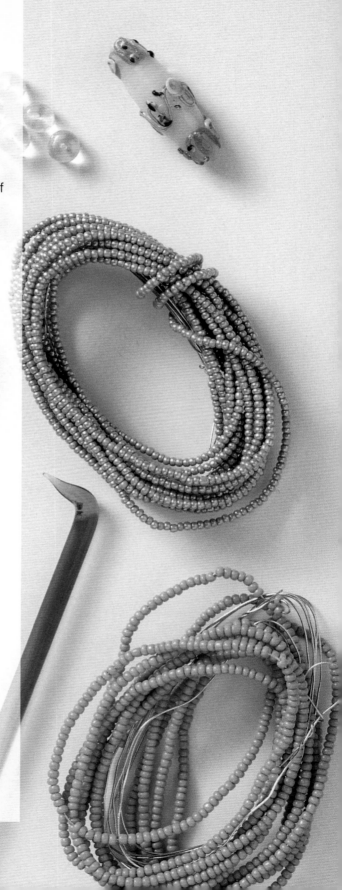

HOW TO STRING BEADS

In order to produce aesthetically pleasing work that will last over time, one must use high quality materials. Plastic beads, while economical, produce disappointing results.

Glass beads of uniform size are preferable. Before starting to string, be sure that you are comfortable and have good lighting.

Spread a light-colored cloth over the work table to prevent beads from rolling to the floor while you work. Pour the beads in a long, shallow bowl with slightly raised sides. Cut 2m (6') of thread. Make a loop at one end and gather and thread the beads, with regular movements, from the top layer of the bowl to the other end of the thread. In this way, the beads string themselves, sliding onto the thread. If you find a blocked hole, open it using a pin or a thinner thread. Once about 130cm (51") of the thread has been strung, tie it off with a loop (the remaining thread will be used later). Roll up each string of beads into a ring as it is finished.

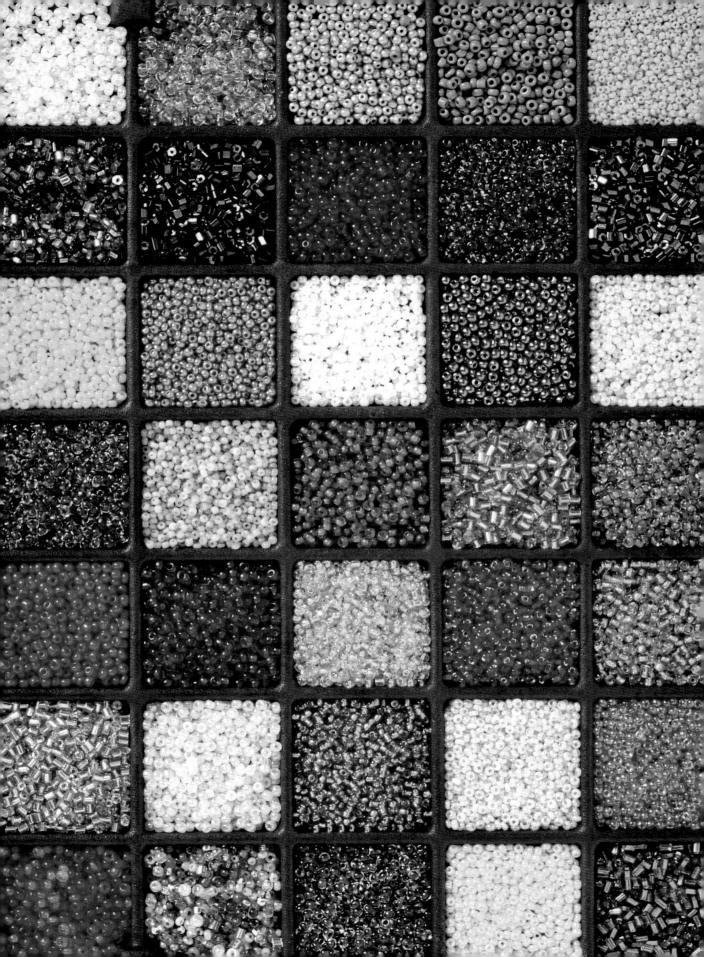

Spools of silk thread
in various colors

Scissors

Craft glue

Iron stems

Spools of zinc-coated wire in various
colors and thickness

TOOLS

Tape
measure

Pliers

Wire cutters

FLOWERS

ROSE

Supplies
- 6-7 strings of beads,
  1.5m (3¹/₂') in length
- zinc-coated wire,
  no. 40 and no. 60
- rigid stem, 60cm (24")
- 2 flexible stems for
  the leaves
- silk thread to match
  bead color
- glue
- pliers and wire
  clippers

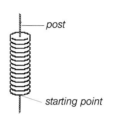

post

starting point

rows

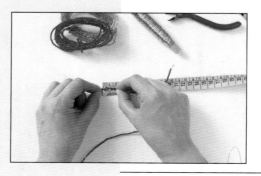

1 – Cut 10cm of
no. 60 wire and string
the beads needed
to make the post.
The post will become
the center of each
petal.

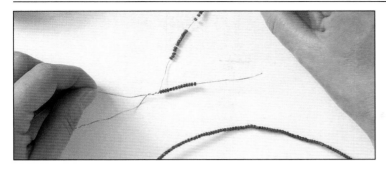

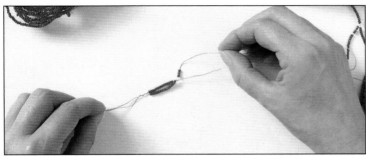

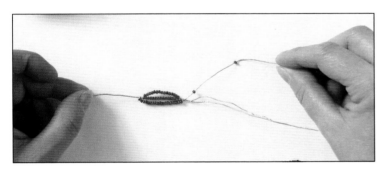

2 – Prepare the strings of beads with no. 40 wire in colors of your choice (in this case, red and gold). Take the post, keeping the beads previously strung at the center, and attach the first length of beads strung on the no. 40 wire around the bottom end of the post, twisting tightly a couple of times.

3 – Start to work the string around the post, attaching the beads around the top end with two tight twists. Continue winding the strings of beads in this way as many times as is necessary to reach the desired petal size.

4 – To create a harmonious petal it is important to make sure that both the front and the back of your work are well done, so be very careful when you wind the wire. With this technique called "the post", you make enough petals for the first corolla (four petals, 2cm ($^7/_8$") in length, winded to make four rows); for the second corolla (four petals, 3cm (1") in length, wound six times); for the third corolla (four petals, 4cm (1$^1/_2$") in length, wound eight times); for the center of the rose (one petal, 2cm ($^7/_8$") in length, wound four times). When all the petals are finished, turn the post over and cut the wires with the wire clippers, leaving about $^1/_2$cm. Using the pliers, bend these ends of the wires closely against the last bead.

5 – To assemble, place the center of the rose against the rigid stem, then wind the wires tightly together using the silk thread ("threading"). Proceed in this manner, using the silk thread to attach the various petals, starting with the smallest, innermost petals and working outward to the largest ones.

6 – Now make the neck of the rose. Prepare five small gold leaves starting with a post of 1.5cm ($^5/_8$"), winding around the post twice using the double point technique (adding two beads at every twist so as to create a point). Twist the string a couple of times around the post, keeping a small distance between each twist. Attach the neck under the last petals of the rose, tying them well with the silk thread. Continue in this manner until the leaves are finished.

7 – Prepare six leaves with a post of 2cm ($^7/_8$") wound to make three rows. On the flexible stem, starting from the top, insert a leaf and begin to tie it off with the silk thread.

8 – Moving toward the bottom, insert the other leaves and, after finishing the threading process, glue the thread to the stem. Continuing to thread, attach the two stems of leaves onto the stem of the rose and thread to the end.

9 – Finish the threading process. Then, use your thumbs to shape the petals and to give the flower a graceful appearance.

DAHLIA

Supplies:
- 7–8 strings of beads
- zinc-coated wire, no. 40 and no. 60
- rigid stem 60cm (24")
- flexible stem
- silk thread to match bead color
- craft glue
- pliers
- wire clippers

Use the post technique. To make the flower you will need: six central petals made from a 1cm ($^3/_8$") post with one row worked around it; six petals made from a 2.5cm (1") post with three rows; and twelve petals made from a 3cm ($1^1/_8$") post with three rows.

1 – For the pistils, string 1cm ($^3/_8$") of beads, string a red bead, then continue to string another 1cm of beads.

2 – With this prepared string, make a loop. Tie it off by twisting the wire together. Repeat to make ten loops.

3 – For the leaves, use the loop technique. Prepare seven leaves, each made of seven loops, 4cm ($1^3/_5$") in length, leaving a space of 0.5cm ($^3/_{16}$") between the loops.

4 – Assemble the flowers. Twist the pistils together at the base and place them against the rigid stem. Thread the pistils onto the stem using the silk thread. One by one, attach each petal using the silk thread. Then, attach the leaves directly to the stem. Continue to cover the length of the stem with silk thread, using a little glue to fix the end of the thread to the stem. Shape the petals of the dahlia.

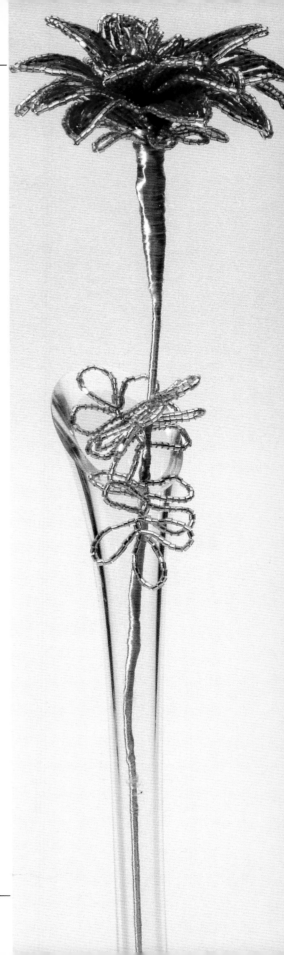

PINK LILY

Supplies:
- strings of glass beads (pink, purple, light green, dark green, glazed white)
- rigid stem 60cm (24")
- flexible stems
- silk thread to match bead color
- zinc-coated wire, no. 60 and no. 50
- craft glue
- pliers
- wire cutters

1 – Cut 15cm of no. 60 wire to make a post and string 3cm (1⅛") of beads onto it.

2 – String pink beads on no. 50 wire to make a petal. At the top, use a double point (each time you wind the string of beads around the post, add a bead and twist the wire around that bead twice. At the bottom, make the petal rounded. Wind the string of beads around the post this way for five rows.

3 – Wind a string of white beads around the pink petal. Make six such petals for every flower. For the pistils, at one end of the wire, string 2cm of purple beads, then twist them into a tight loop. At the other end string 6–7cm of light green beads. Make six or seven pistils and tie them together with the thinner wire.

4 – Assemble the flowers. At the end of the rigid stem, attach the pistils with silk thread and glue. Attach the six petals; thread for 6–7cm (2–3") and attach a leaf. Attach flowers, leaves and buds onto the flexible stems to make small branches. Attach these to the rigid stem.

IRIS

Supplies:
- 6-7 strings of different colored beads
- zinc-coated wire no. 60
- rigid stem, 40cm (16")
- silk thread to match bead color
- craft glue
- pliers
- wire cutters

Make six petals, starting each with a 3cm (1⅛") post, then wind seven rows in alternating colors. As you wind the second row, make the loops parallel to the post to produce petals with a wide base. Make three yellow anthers using a double point with a 3cm (1⅛") post wound around in one row and another three anthers with 3cm (1⅛") posts wound around in two rows.

1 – Prepare the center pistils making a 4cm (1⅗") long loop, bringing the string of beads through the loop's middle. Roll it at the base and twist it around itself; cut loose ends of wire.

2 – Position the pistil at the end of a stem along with one petal and attach them with silk thread.

3 – With silk thread, assemble the inner petals, the outer ones and the anther at center.

4 – Thread the stem for 3–4cm (1⅛–1⅗"), then attach the three double-pointed anthers of the same color as the center ones. Use glue to keep the thread firmly attached. Shape the flower by curving its upper petals toward the center and curving the others downward. Cover the stem with silk thread for about 20cm (8"), then attach the two green leaves made with posts of 14–15cm (5⅗–6") with three rows of thread.

ICE CRYSTALS

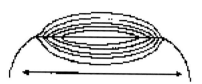

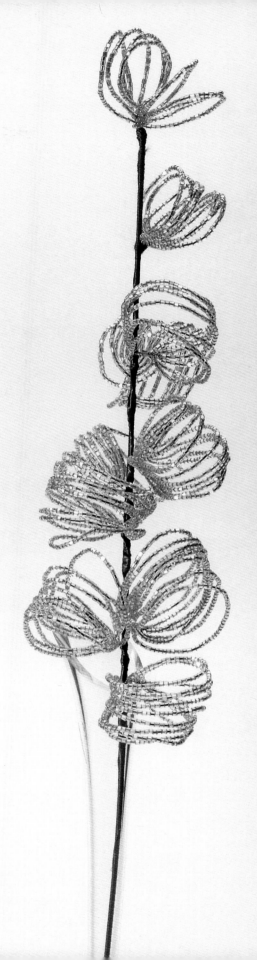

Supplies:
- various silver bead strings
- zinc-coated wire, no. 50
- rigid stem, 40cm (16")
- silk thread to match bead color
- craft glue
- pliers
- wire cutters

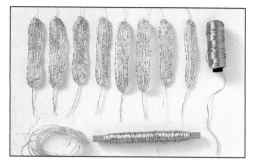

1 – Cut about 10cm of zinc-coated wire (no. 50). String 9cm (3¹/₂") of beads, keeping them at post center. Wind the string in nine rows around the post, twisting them tightly around the wire so that the strings of beads are parallel.

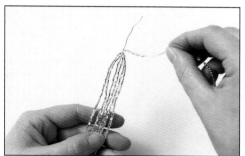

2 – After you make eight or nine leaves, bend them in half and shape them delicately until rounded.

3 – Take the rigid stem and attach the first leaf to it with silk thread. Leaving a space of about 5cm (2"), attach another leaf. Continue until all the leaves are attached. Leave about 20cm (8") of stem at the bottom which will be also covered by silk thread.

TULIP

Supplies:
- 3–4 strings of beads in different colors
- rigid stem, 40cm (16")
- zinc-coated wire, no. 40 and no. 60
- silk thread to match bead color
- craft glue
- tweezers
- wire cutters

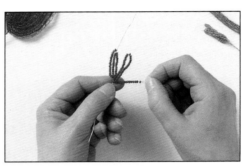

1 – Make four petals with 4cm (1³/₅") posts in seven rows. For each petal, make a loop at each end after the first row to create a wide-form base and a pointed tip.

2 – For the central pistil, make two 4cm (1³/₅") loops next to one another and wrap them together in a spiral. For the center, make a fringe of ten loops of different sizes (3, 4, and 5cm) (1¹/₅, 1³/₅, and 2").

3 – Using tweezers, continue to round out the petal, curving the two parallel loops to the post.

4 – At the top of the rigid stem, attach the pistil, already attached to the fringe of loops. Twist tightly and start to thread. Then attach the four petals, closing them together to achieve a cup-like form. Continue to wrap the silk thread around the stem, also attaching the two leaves which are made with 14-16cm (5³/₅–6²/₅") posts wound in three rows.

FREESIA

Supplies:
- *strings of beads in different colors*
- *zinc-coated wire, no. 50 and no. 60*
- *silk thread to match bead color*
- *craft glue*
- *flexible stem*
- *pliers*
- *wire cutters*

Make each bough with two or three equally large flowers, two large buds, two medium buds, two small buds, a looped bud and a leaf.

Large bud (3 petals): Each petal starts with a 1cm post. Wind the strung beads twice around the post, forming a petal that is rounded at the top and elongated toward the bottom.

Medium bud (3 petals): Make a 0.5cm post and follow the instructions above.

Small bud (3 petals): With a post of 0.5cm, wind once, rounded at the top, elongated at the bottom.

Looped bud: Make a loop of 4cm ($^2/_5$") and bend it in half.

Leaf: On a post insert 5–6cm (2–2$^2/_5$") of beads and wind it for two rows using a double point.

1 – Large flower, made with three outer, and three inner petals, pistils and calyx. For the outer petals, on a 10cm post of no. 50 wire, string 3cm (1$^1/_8$") of beads. Round the upper tip and elongate the petal's lower part (use triple stitch).

2 – To triple-stitch, wind the string of beads in three rows, leaving distance between the rows to lengthen the petal. Wind three rows for the three petals. For the inner petals, string 2cm ($^4/_5$") of beads on the post and wind around the post for two rows. For the pistils, string 5cm (2") of beads and bend in half to make a 2.5cm (1") loop; make three of these loops. For the calyx make five loops, each 3cm (1$^1/_8$") long, using the daisy technique. Assemble the large flower by threading the pistils

together, and then attach the three inner petals and the three large petals with the silk thread. Lastly, attach the calyx, which is threaded for 1cm ($^3/_8$").

3 – To assemble the bough, attach the looped bud at the top of the stem threading for 2cm ($^4/_5$"). Attach the buds and the large flowers with the silk thread. Lastly, attach the bough and the green leaves onto another stem.

NARCISSUS

Supplies:
- 4–5 strings of beads
- zinc-coated wire, no. 50
- rigid stem
- silk thread to match bead color
- craft glue
- pliers
- wire cutters

Make six petals with a 2cm (⁴/₅") post wound for three rows using the double point technique which consists of winding the strings of beads a couple of times around the post, keeping a slight distance between them. Then prepare three petals with a 1.5cm (³/₅") post wound for two rows using the double point in order to make the calyx. Finally, create a leaf with a 14–15cm (5³/₅–6") post wound for three rows.

1 – For the crown, measure 5cm (2") of strung beads and bend them in half to make a loop. Twist the wire to secure the loop at the base. Make ten loops.

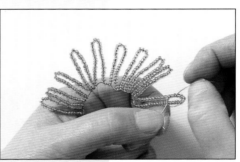

2 – Fasten a piece of wire under the fifth bead of the first loop. String a bead onto the wire and wrap the end of the wire under the fifth bead on the other side of the loop. String another bead onto the wire and continue entering the next loop under its fifth bead, and so on until all the loops are done.

3 – Twist the two ends of the wires together, pulling the wire at the base to tighten the circle formed by the loops.

4 – Make the central pistil. With a small string of beads, make three little loops close together, wrap the wire around the loops to fasten them off and then string onto the wire a few more beads. Wind this around the base again.

5 – Insert the pistil in the flower's crown. Attach both onto the rigid stem with the silk thread.

6 – Add the six petals, fastening with the silk thread. Beneath the petals,

cover 5cm (2") of stem with the thread before adding the three double-pointed petals of the calyx.

7 – Continue to thread the stem. Add the leaf directly onto the rigid stem.

8 – With pliers, slightly bend the corolla of the flower forward. Gracefully shape the petals that form the calyx.

GENTIAN

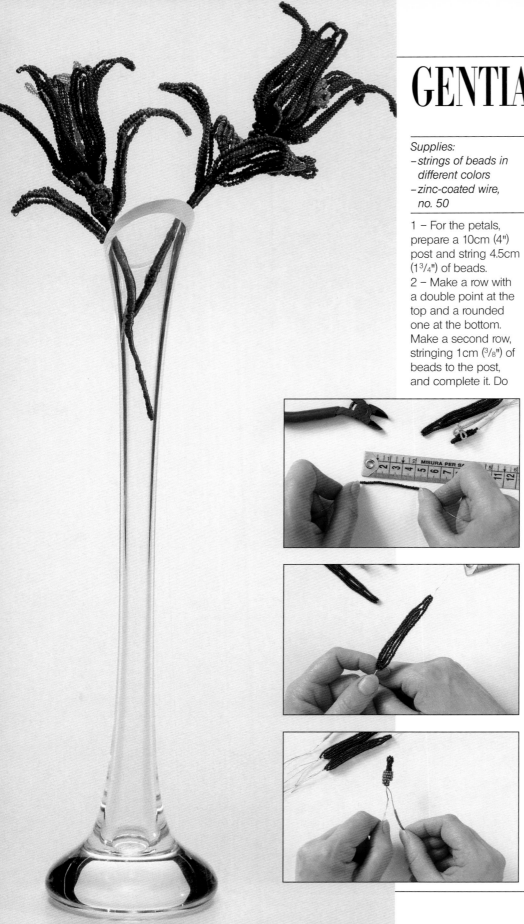

Supplies:
- strings of beads in different colors
- zinc-coated wire, no. 50
- flexible stem
- silk thread to match bead color
- craft glue
- wire cutters

1 – For the petals, prepare a 10cm (4") post and string 4.5cm (1³/₄") of beads.

2 – Make a row with a double point at the top and a rounded one at the bottom. Make a second row, stringing 1cm (³/₈") of beads to the post, and complete it. Do not cut the post, but turn it, from backside to front and cut it close to the bead string. Make five petals.

3 – For the bud, make three loops, each 2.5cm (1") (measure 5cm (2") of strung beads and bend them in half), and twist them together. With green bead string, starting at the bud's center, form a calyx, down to the base. Secure the wire and cut.

For the central pistils, measure 2.5cm (1") of beads. At the top make three small loops. Twist them together three times. Bring down 2.5cm (1") of strung beads and tie the two wires together. For the leaves, string 4.5cm (1³/₄") of beads on the post and wind rows around the post using the double point at the top and rounded at the base. Making the second row, string 2cm (⁴/₅") of beads on the post to give an elongated form.

For the base of the calyx, make five loops of 1.5cm (³/₅") and fasten it off in a ring.

On a stem, attach pistils, petals and the base of the calyx with silk thread. Wrap the stem with thread for another 4–5cm (1⁴/₅–2"), then attach the buds and the leaves.

POPPY

Supplies:
- *strings of beads (red, black, green or red and gold)*
- *zinc-coated wire, no. 60*
- *rigid stem*
- *flexible stems*
- *silk thread to match bead color*
- *craft glue*
- *pliers*
- *wire cutters*

Prepare four petals on a post of 1.5cm (³/₅"), wound seven times, to achieve a rounded form. Be precise to make the petals very round.

Make some leaves with a post of 2cm (⁴/₅") wound for four rows. Shape the last turn into the typical serrated form.

For the bud, use the post technique: make a petal with a 1.5cm (³/₅") post wound for three rows with a string of red beads, and wind one row with a contrasting color. For the bud's green leaf, make a 2cm (⁴/₅") post wound for three rows.

1 – For the flower's center, prepare six loops, each with six beads and wrap them around to look like a button.

2 – Build around them ten loops 2.5cm (1") long to form the pistils.

3 – To assemble the flower, attach two leaves onto the rigid stem. On a flexible stem, attach the bud. With silk thread and glue, attach the button and, under it, the pistils to the rigid stem. Firmly attach the four petals with the silk thread. Thread the stem for another 4-5cm (2"), then attach the bud stem. Finish covering the stem with thread.

PEONY

Supplies:
- *strings of beads in different colors*
- *zinc-coated wire, no. 40 and no. 50*
- *flexible stems*
- *rigid stem*
- *silk thread to match bead color*
- *craft glue*
- *pliers*
- *wire cutters*

Make the peony with nine or ten outer petals, four central petals, some loops for the pistils, four buds and four leaves.

Prepare the nine outer petals with a 2cm ($^4/_5$") post wound for eight rows for a rounded petal. On the last row, use a contrasting color.

Make the four leaves each with a double point at the top of the leaf and rounded at the bottom. For an elongated form, on each row, add two beads to the post. To make the buds, roll a petal around itself in a spiral effect.

1 – For the central petals, measure 2cm of wire for the post and work around four rows, plus a fifth row in a contrasting color.

2 – Once the petal is finished, bend the post backward and cut it with the wire clippers a half centimeter from the base. Make three other petals in the same way.

3 – For the pistils, make a loop with 3cm (1$^1/_8$") of strung beads, bend and fasten it off at the base without cutting the wire. Make three others this way.

4 – To assemble the flower, attach the pistils with silk thread onto the rigid stem. Add the small petals and attach with silk thread, then the outer petals, and so on. Use glue to firmly attach the petals to the stem during threading. Lastly, add the four leaves and the buds, mounted separately onto flexible stems.

LILY

Supplies:
- strings of beads (white, gold, and green)
- rigid stem, 60cm (2')
- flexible stems
- zinc-coated wire, no. 40 and no. 60
- large crystals for pistils
- silk thread to match bead color
- craft glue
- pliers
- wire cutters

Prepare seven petals with the post technique. For each petal, use 6cm (2²/₅") of wire on which you string 4cm (1³/₅") of beads. Work in double point at the top and rounded at the bottom for four rows. Then, outline the petal in a contrasting color for three rows. To do this, cut off the string of beads at the petal's base and insert a new string, tied securely at the base.

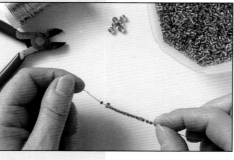

1 – For the pistils, string on a wire with 4cm (1³/₅") of beads, a crystal and a single bead.

2 – String the wire again through the crystal and some other beads.

3 – Cut the wire and set it aside until it is time to attach the bundle of pistils.

4 – Take a 10–12cm (4–4³/₄") string of beads, with a partially empty piece of wire, and bend the wire in half. Make two loops near each other and tie them together. Then twist the two parts of the string of beads that hang from the loops.

5 – Make three or four pistils, then gather them together and tie them to form a bundle.

6 – To make the bud, wrap a petal around itself to give it a conical shape. Do the same with the leaf, placing it at the base of the bud.

To assemble the flower, attach the bundle of pistils onto the rigid stem using the silk thread and a little glue. Add the six petals, forming them into a funnel shape. Thread the stem for 5–6cm (2–2²/₅"), then add the bud and a small leaf. Wrap the rest of the stem with thread. Use a little glue to keep the thread firmly in place.

Lastly, shape the petals and bend them slightly downward to give the lilies their classic shape.

POINSETTAS

Supplies:
- strings of red and green beads
- crystals for the pistils
- zinc-coated wire, gold
- flexible stems
- silk thread
- craft glue
- pliers
- wire cutters

Make four petals with a 1.5cm (³/₅") post wound for two rows using the double point at both top and bottom of the petals. Then, make another twelve petals with a 2.5cm (1") post wound for two rows, using the double point. Make three leaves using a 1.5cm (³/₅") post wound three rows using the double point.

1 – For the pistils, string a crystal on the wire and, at the base, wrap the wire around itself.

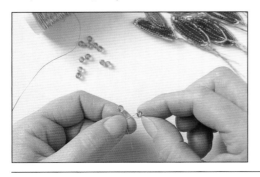

2 – Without cutting the wire, string another crystal and repeat the operation.

3 – Proceed in this way until you form a bundle of eight pistils.

4 – To assemble, firmly attach the pistils onto a flexible stem with the silk thread. Thread four petals onto the stem. Arrange the other petals, slightly overlapping, and attach with the thread. Attach the green leaves and finish covering the stem with thread.

CAMELLIA

Supplies:
- string of beads, both normal and glazed in chosen colors
- zinc-coated wire, white, no. 60 and no. 50
- flexible stems
- silk thread to match bead color
- pliers
- wire cutters

Make nine petals and three leaves. For each petal, string 1.5cm ($^3/_5$") of beads onto a post (no. 50 wire) and work around the post five times for rounded petals. For each leaf, string 3.5cm ($1^2/_5$") of glazed glass beads onto a post (no. 60 wire) and work around for five rows using double point.

1 – For the sprigs, take 4cm ($1^3/_5$") of strung beads. Bend the string in half and make a loop.

2 – Make two other loops next to each other. Wrap the two ends of wire into a tight cord and continue to make four groups, each having three loops. Make two sprigs.

3 - Roll up a petal to make the flower's center. Attach it to a flexible stem, using silk thread. Attach the other petals, three leaves and two sprigs. Cover 5–6cm ($1^4/_5$–$2^2/_5$") of stem with thread. Roll up the stem.

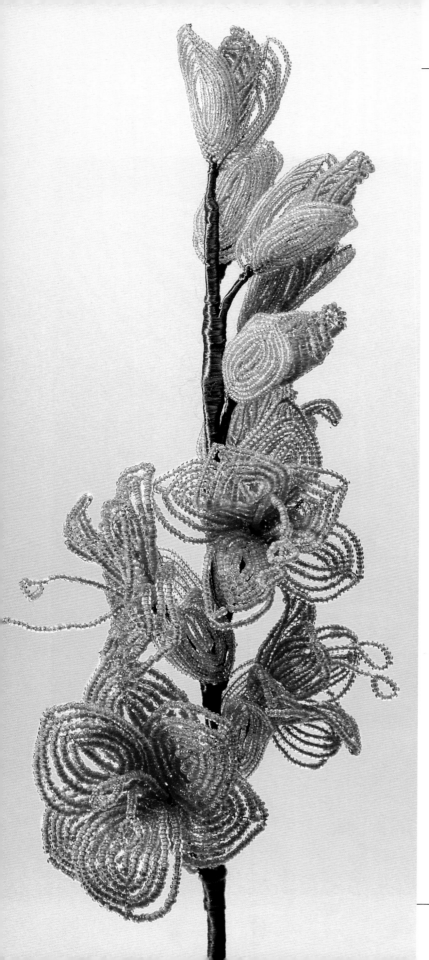

GLADIOLA

Necessary elements to make:

– A large flower:
Four petals with a 2cm ($^4/_5$") post wound five times; add two beads to elongate the last row. Two petals with a 2cm ($^4/_5$") post wound four times; add two beads to elongate the last row. Two pistils made from a 3cm ($1^1/_8$") string of beads with a 1cm ($^3/_8$") loop at the tip. Two leaves with a 1.5cm ($^3/_5$") post strung with small green beads, wound six times with double point.

– A small flower:
Six petals with a 2cm ($^4/_5$") post wound four times; add two beads to elongate the last row. Two or three pistils made from 2.5cm (1") of strung beads with a loop at each tip. Two leaves with a 1.5cm ($3^1/_2$") post wound six times using the double point.

– Two flowers with four petals:
Four petals with a 2cm ($^7/_8$") post wound four times; add two beads to elongate the last row.

– Three large buds:
First twisted petal from a 2cm ($^7/_8$") post wound seven times, plus two leaves from a 2cm post wound six times.

– Three small buds:
Twisted petal with a 1.5cm ($3^1/_2$") post wound four times, plus two leaves from a 1.5cm post wound five times.

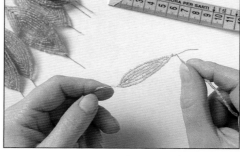

Supplies:
- strings of beads in different colors
- very small green beads for leaves
- zinc-coated wire, no. 50
- rigid and flexible stems
- silk thread to match bead color
- craft glue
- wire cutters

1 – For each petal of the large flower, prepare a 20cm (8") wire post and string 2cm ($^4/_5$") of beads onto it.

2 – Work around for five rows using the double point at top and bottom (in the last row, add two beads at the top).

3 – For the buds, follow the instructions to make the petals, then roll them around a finger, to shape them and give them roundness.

4 – To assemble the single flowers, use the silk thread to attach the pistils to the end of a flexible stem. Add petals to make the corolla, and shape them. Cover the stem with thread for several inches. To add the buds, thread the twisted petal on the rigid stem; add two leaves and thread for a couple of inches. To assemble the sprig, attach the first bud onto a 60cm (2') stem, using silk thread and glue. Follow the same process for all the others, attaching both large and small flowers.

With the same technique as the gladiola, you can create a stem of orchids (right).

DAISY

Supplies:
- strings of beads in different colors
- zinc-coated wire, no. 50
- rigid stems (40cm, 16")
- silk thread to match bead color
- craft glue
- pliers
- wire cutters

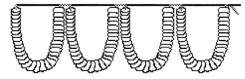

1 – This flower must be worked directly from the string of beads. Start by leaving 15–20cm (6–8") of wire free, then string 8cm ($^5/_{16}$") with beads and make the first loop that you will fasten off by winding it around the base.

2 – String another 8cm ($^5/_{16}$") of beads and, with your left hand, holding the loop you have just made, make another loop, wrapping the string of beads around the empty wire in a complete circle.

3 – Continue in this way until you have made nine loops, each of them 8cm ($^5/_{16}$") long. These must be fastened by winding the wire a couple of times; however, they must be left free to slide so that they can be easily curled at the end.

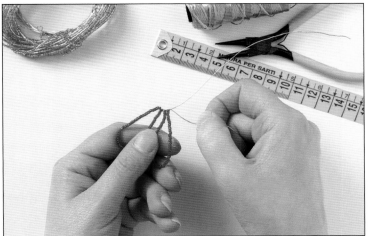

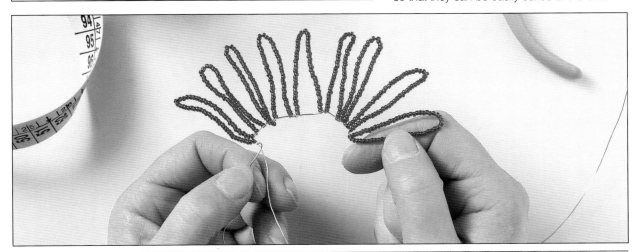

4 – Make the return row: holding the first series of loops with your left hand, insert a loop in the middle of the base of each of the preceding ones. Once all the loops are made, pull the wire to curl the petals.

5 – To make the neck of the flower, use the same technique as above to prepare six loops, each having about ten beads. When done, pull the wire slightly to gather them.

6 – For the center of the flower, make 15 loops of eight to ten beads each, wrapping them like a button.

7 – For the leaves, make a loop and fasten it at the base; let a few beads slide down the wire, wrap it off and fasten it again.

8 – Make some more loops, both to the right and to the left of the string of beads from which you are making the branch and gradually increase the length.

9 – To assemble, thread the center of the flower in the opening formed after you gathered the petal loops and join it together by inserting the stem; fasten it with thread and a little glue to keep the work together.

10 – Insert the neck at the base of the petals, continuing to cover the stem with silk thread. Attach the leaves directly to the stem.

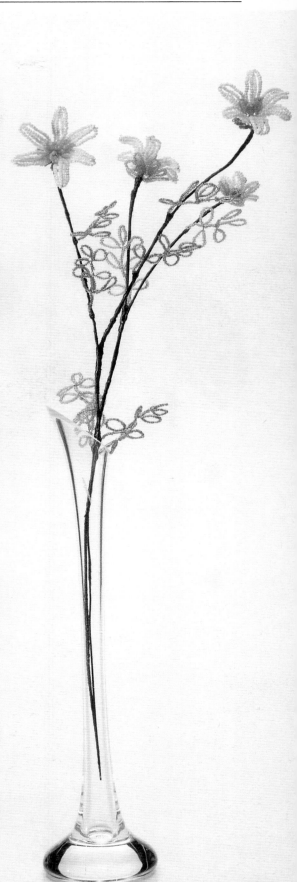

CYCLAMENS

Supplies:
- *4–5 strings of beads in various shades of dark pink*
- *2–3 strings of beads*
- *in various shades of green*
- *flexible stems*
- *zinc-coated wire, no. 50*
- *silk thread to match bead color*
- *craft glue*
- *pliers*
- *wire cutters*

1 – Prepare a string of beads in different shades of dark pink on a 20cm length of wire. Leave the first bit free and work directly on the string of beads, creating five loops, each having 15 beads. Fasten them off at the base by wrapping the wire around a couple of times, but leave them loose enough so that they can be pulled and gathered.

2 – Go back and make five petals, using 3cm (1¹⁄₈") of strung beads, over the petals you have already made. Fasten off all the loops, pull the wire slightly and gather the petals. Give the second row of beads a pointed shape, bending them slightly upward.

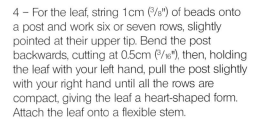

3 – Wind the ends of the wire together to make a stem.

4 – For the leaf, string 1cm (³⁄₈") of beads onto a post and work six or seven rows, slightly pointed at their upper tip. Bend the post backwards, cutting at 0.5cm (³⁄₁₆"), then, holding the leaf with your left hand, pull the post slightly with your right hand until all the rows are compact, giving the leaf a heart-shaped form. Attach the leaf onto a flexible stem.

To assemble, attach each little flower to the flexible stem, using thread and a little glue. Then attach the leaves. Cover the entire length of the stem with the silk thread.

In order to create a bouquet of various colors, attach all the stems together, with thread, onto a flexible stem.

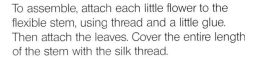

STALKS OF WHEAT

Supplies:
- strings of beads in different sizes
- zinc-coated wire, no. 40
- zinc-coated wire, yellow
- rigid stems
- silk thread to match bead color
- craft glue
- pliers
- wire cutters

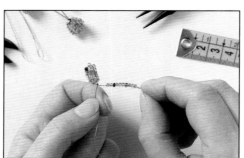

1 – String 2cm of beads onto wire, then make a loop. Winding it around itself, bend the loop in half and pass it back, crossing through in the opposite direction. In this way, you have created a double loop.

2 – Wind the wire at the base of the double loop to secure it firmly.

3 – Without cutting the wire, make a second double loop, once again using 2cm (⁴/₅") of strung beads.

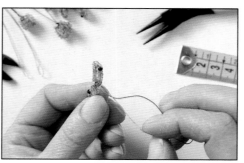

4 – Twist the ends of the wire hanging from the double loops to fasten them off. Then cut off the excess wire.

5 – You have made two grains of wheat. Continue working in this way until you have made 20 couples of grain.

6 – Now prepare the rest of the stalks. Cut 20 pieces of yellow wire, 30cm each, and bend them in half.

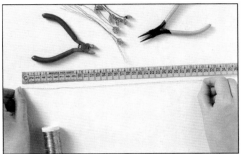

7 – On a rigid stem, attach a string with the silk thread. Continue wrapping with the thread for 0.5cm ($^3/_{16}$").

8 – After the first string, attach a grain of wheat and continue wrapping the thread for 0.5cm ($^3/_{16}$").

9 – Turn the piece onto the other side and attach another string and a grain, continuing to wrap the thread. Proceed in this way until you have used up all the strings and grain.

With the same technique you can make stalks of lavender. You make double kernels and attach them with the thread, as described above for the grain, adding small leaves directly onto the stem.

MIMOSA

Supplies:
- *beads in various shades of yellow and green*
- *zinc-coated wire, no. 40*
- *rigid stems*
- *silk thread to match bead color*
- *craft glue*
- *pliers*
- *wire cutters*

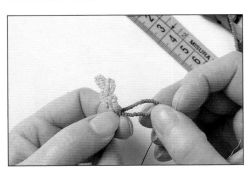

Begin by stringing a few yellow beads onto the wire, then leave about 25-30cm of wire unstrung.

1 – Make a loop of eight beads (about 2cm of strung wire). Wind it around itself and finish it off by braiding it at the base. Twist the hanging wires for about 0.5cm.

2 – Make another couple of loops, staggered in relation to the other.

3 – Insert the string of green beads and make a number of loops of varying length, continuing to twist the wires to give the appearance of a stem, onto which small leaves are entwined. Cut all the wires.

4 – Create different little stems, filling them with leaves and little flowers in various shades of yellow.

To assemble, attach the first little stem onto a rigid main stem using the silk thread. Then attach the others, arranging the flowers and leaves. Continue to wrap the thread, using some glue, until you cover the entire length of the stem.

FORSYTHIA

Supplies:
- strings of yellow and green beads
- zinc-coated wire, no. 40
- rigid stems
- silk thread to match bead color
- craft glue
- pliers
- wire cutters

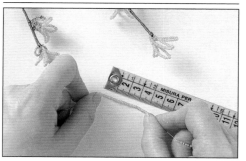

1 – Prepare a string of beads and leave 4-5cm of wire unstrung. Bend 4cm (1³/₅") of beads in half to make a loop, then make three more.

2 – The loops must be fastened well at the base by wrapping the wire around twice. The loops must be left loose enough so that they can be pulled and gathered. Do not cut the wires.

3 – Leaving 4cm of wire unstrung, create a new little flower and then, with the same wire, make another six or seven flowers.

4 – Separately, with the string of green beads, make two loops, which must be positioned under the first little flower. Maintaining the same distance left previously for the flowers, create many small green loops which, during the assembly, will be positioned to form the calyx.

Assemble the flower to the calyx using the silk thread firmly onto the tip of a stem. Proceed in the same way until you have made an entire stem.

PEACH BLOSSOMS

Supplies:
- *bead strings of different sizes in shades of pink, green, and yellow*
- *zinc-coated wire, no. 40*
- *silk thread to match bead color*
- *flexible stems and rigid stems or peach tree branches with small buds*
- *craft glue*
- *pliers*
- *wire cutters*

For every stem it is necessary to make numerous small flowers that you can fashion with the loop technique (five loops for every flower for three rows) or with the post technique. If you use the post technique, cut a piece of wire, insert four beads at the center and, with the string of beads, work around three rows to make five rounded petals. Once each petal is finished, cut the wires after they have been fastened off well at the base of the post.

For the pistils, make a small ring with the wire and string 3cm (1 1/8") of small beads. Cut the wire after 4cm (1 3/5") and make four or five pistils; then, wrap the wire around the base to hold them together.

To make the small leaves, cut a piece of green wire and string 1.5cm of small beads of the same color. With the string of beads, work two rows around the post.

1 – To assemble the flower, attach the pistils onto the stem using the silk thread. Then, attach the five petals and continue to wrap the thread around the stem a couple of times.

2 – Now add a small leaf and continue to wrap with the thread.

3 – Finish off by using a little glue to fasten the thread.

During the assembling process attach to the rigid stem or the branch of peach a small leaf among the individual flowers every so often.

WATERLILY

Supplies:
- *strings of pink, white; strings of glazed beads and green beads for the leaves*
- *zinc-coated wire, no. 50*
- *silk thread to match bead color*
- *crystals for the pistils*
- *craft glue*
- *pliers*
- *wire cutters*

Two techniques may be used to make the waterlily—the loop technique or the post technique. Either one yields beautiful results. Basically, the choice of colors, equally brilliant and delicate, and the arrangement of bead types, from the classic to the glazed to crystals, create eye-pleasing contrasts.

For the waterlily made with the loop technique, pink and white beads are recommended.

1 – Make the first row of petals with the white string of beads: five 1.5cm (³/₅") loops made with 3cm (1¹/₈") of strung beads bent in two. These must be secured well by winding the wire a couple of times, but must be left loose enough to slide pulling and gathering. Make the second row using the string of pink beads to make ten loops of 3cm (1¹/₈"). When the loops are finished, take the wire around and fasten it. Cut it, leaving a tail.

2 – Attach the string of white beads onto the piece that was cut off and make a return row of loops, inserting the loop in the middle of the pink loop's base. With the same technique make the third row of petals with 11 loops, each 4cm (1³/₅") in length.
For the fourth row make six double loops, each 3cm (1¹/₈") in length, to form six petals. For the row that forms the base of the flower, make three loops, each 2cm (⁴/₅") in length.

For the pistils, make five or six loops of 1cm (³/₈") in length (2cm, ⁴/₅" bent in half), stringing crystals on the wire.

3 – To assemble the flower, start with the pistils and, step by step, attach the rows, each inside the center hole of the other. At the end, attach the three small loops that form the flower's base. Wrap with the silk thread for 2cm, cut the hanging ends of wire and, using pliers, tuck under the wire stubs.

For the white waterlily outlined in glazed beads, use the post technique. For the first row, make three petals out of 0.5cm (³/₁₆") of strung beads on a rigid post (no. 50). Work three rows making a rounded petal, and add the string of glazed beads to create a contrasting border. For the second row make three petals out of a 1cm (³/₈") post, working four rounded rows plus a row in the opposite direction.
For the third row make four petals out of a 1cm (³/₈") post, working six rounded rows plus a contrasting row. For the fourth row make five petals from a 1cm (³/₈") post, working eight rounded rows plus a contrasting row.
Make two leaves from a 1cm (³/₈") post, working ten rows, and another two leaves from a 0.5cm (³/₁₆") post, working 11 rows.
For the pistils, make five yellow loops, each 2cm (⁴/₅") in length, and twist them.
Assemble the waterlily as you would any flower, but without the stem.

ANEMONE AND LILY OF THE VALLEY

Supplies:
- strings of beads in various colors
- very small white beads
- flexible stems
- zinc-coated wire, no. 40
- silk thread to match bead color
- craft glue
- pliers
- wire cutters

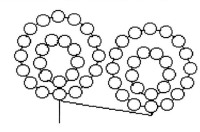

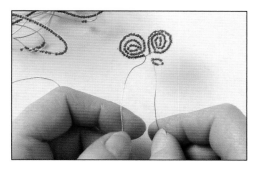

1 – To make the anemone, work with the circle technique, which is as follows. Make a loop of 2cm ($^4/_5$") and wrap it around itself. Continue working the string of beads around the first loop for two rows, securing the wire at the base of each row. Without cutting the wire and remaining fairly near the first petal, make another four petals.

2 – Join them together at the base

to form a corolla. For the pistil make a post of 1cm ($^3/_8$") of strung beads and make two rows around. Insert the pistil into the center of the corolla and attach it onto a stem with silk thread. Wrap the thread all the way to the end of the stem. With this system, you can make lots of flowers of different colors to form a pretty bouquet of anemones.

3 – With the same technique and the same methods of construction, you can create the

petals for lilies of the valley. Make the central loop with 1cm ($^3/_8$") of strung beads. When you make the second row around the first loop, widen it slightly. Create eight flowers, each with four rounded petals made from two rows of beads.

The leaves are made with a 5cm (2") of post worked around for three rows, pointed at the top and rounded at the base.

To assemble the lilies of the valley, first attach the single flowers onto small pieces of flexible stems with silk thread to create a stalk. Then attach the stalks, starting at the tip of a rigid stem, inserting seven or eight on each sprig. At the end, shape the entire composition with pliers.

PRIMROSE

Supplies:
- *strings of beads in various colors*
- *zinc-coated wire, no. 40*
- *flexible stems*
- *silk thread to match bead color*
- *craft glue*
- *pliers*
- *wire cutters*

1 – With the circle technique, tie four or five beads in a circle. Then, without cutting the wire, make another, slightly wider, row around the base of the beads.

2 – Once the five petals are formed, tie the two ends of the wire together. Prepare a number of small flowers this way.

3 – For the bud, make a loop of 1.5cm ($^3/_5$")—3cm ($1^1/_8$") of strung beads bent in half. Close the loop at the base; then, intertwine the string of beads in the middle of the loop, winding it in a spiral.

4 – For the pistil, insert a bead in the center of the post, and, with the string of beads, make a row all around the bead without cutting the wire.

5 – Bend the post well on the backside of the pistil and insert the two wires into the center of the flower; twist off the wire ends at the base.

6 – For the neck of the flower, prepare three small loops of 1cm ($^3/_8$") each.

7 – Attach the three small loops to the base of the flower.

8 – For the leaves, string beads of different shades of green onto a 2.5cm (1") post. Make the leaves rounded at the top and elongated at the bottom, making four rows. If you like, use a darker shade of green for the last row. Make four or five leaves.

To assemble, attach each flower, bud and leaf onto small pieces of stems using silk thread. Put the different pieces together into a single stem, making a bunch of flowers.

VIOLET

Supplies:
- strings of beads in various shades of purple, yellow, and green
- zinc-coated wire, no. 40
- rigid stems
- silk thread to match bead color
- craft glue
- pliers
- wire cutters

The violets can be made with superimposed loops (always with five rows) as in the cluster on the opposite page, or with the circle technique as in the case of the violet illustrated in the step-by-step instructions below.

1 – Make the two upper petals with a string of purple beads. For each petal, make a circle of nine beads and close it without cutting the wire.

2 – Work around for three rows, slightly widening each row. Without cutting, make an identical second petal.
In the same way, make the three lower petals (always attached), slightly larger then the previous ones, using the yellow beads. For the pistils, string a large bead on a piece of wire and twist the two hanging ends together.

3 – For the neck of the flower, make three small loops with a string of green beads. For the leaves, string 2cm (⁴/₅") of beads onto a post. Work seven rows in double point at the top and rounded at the bottom. Gently pull the post so that the rows of beads collect at the center, giving the leaf a heart shape.

4 – To assemble the violet, attach the two upper petals on the stem using the silk thread. Then, still using the silk thread, attach the pistil, the three lower petals and lastly, the three loops for the neck. Continue to wrap the stem with thread for another 10cm (4").

Now you can create a bouquet of different flowers and, if you wish, attach some small green leaves at the base for a finishing touch.

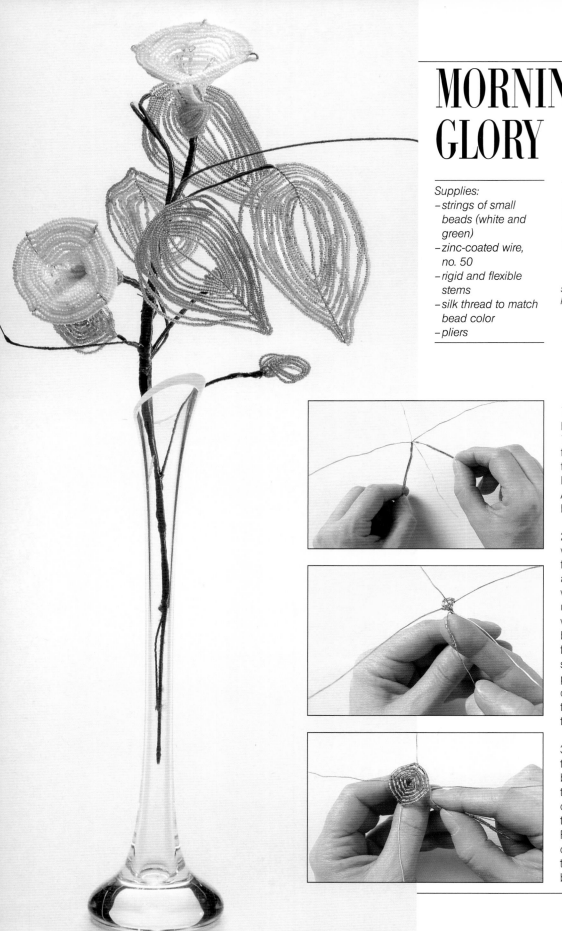

MORNING GLORY

Supplies:
- *strings of small beads (white and green)*
- *zinc-coated wire, no. 50*
- *rigid and flexible stems*
- *silk thread to match bead color*
- *pliers*

To create this delicate flower, use the completely new "crossed-posts" technique.

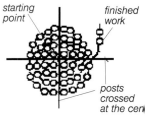

starting point
finished work
posts crossed at the cen[ter]

1 – Prepare four pieces of wire about 15–16cm long. Join them at one end by twisting half of their lengths together. Attach a string of beads.

2 – Open the four wires so that they form separate rays and, holding the base with your left hand, use your right hand to wind the string of beads around the four wires (which should function as posts). String a bead on each wire, so that the winding stays on the backside.

3 – Continue filling the four spaces with beads, widening the rows until you obtain a flower of the desired size. Fasten off the string of beads well, bend the wire on the backside and cut it.

4 – Bend the four posts backwards, cover them with beads and fasten them to the flower's base. Shape the flower into the form of a funnel.

5 – Attach a rigid stem to the flower's base and wind the silk thread around it with some glue.

6 – Cover the entire stem. Then, form the calyx by wrapping a string of beads around the stem and forming two rows of beads at the base of the flower.

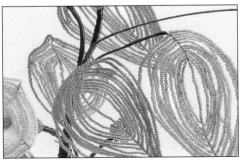

7 – Make five leaves, rounded at bottom and in double point at top (3cm, 1 1/8" post for nine rows of strung beads). Wrap silk thread around each flexible stem. Attach the flowers with silk thread and add leaves.

GRAPES

Supplies:
- strings of small beads in selected colors
- zinc-coated wire, no. 50
- flexible and rigid stems
- silk thread to match bead color
- pliers
- wire cutters

1 – Cut four pieces of wire and cross them, tying them at the base with a string of beads. Beginning at the center, add a bead in the first row and cross the posts so that you see only continuous lines of beads on the right side of the work. Add two beads in the second row, add three in the third row and add four in the fourth

row, using your fingers to give the piece the characteristic shape of a grape.

2 – Once you have achieved the desired size of the grape, begin to take away beads from each row in order to taper the grape.

3 – Wind the wire of each row around itself. Make twenty or more of these grapes according to the dimensions you wish to give the bunch.

4 – To make the vine leaves, start with a small loop of strung beads so the beads cannot slide off. Then, wind it in a spiral onto a rigid stem.

5 – Finish winding, leaving a piece of wire free around the last two or three beads to secure them. Leave about 10cm of wire (which will be used later to assemble the bunch); then, cut the excess wire.

6 – After you have threaded the grapes, begin to assemble the bunch. Starting at the tip of a flexible stem, attach the first grape and, always using the silk thread, attach the vine leaves and the leaves you have already prepared, putting them together three at a time (of the type with the double point at the top and rounded at the bottom) with small hidden stitches. Arrange the grapes to form a bunch, pulling the vine leaves, as if they were springs, and shaping the leaves.

SUNFLOWER

Before making this flower, prepare a number of strings of beads, 10m (11yds) in total. Use the crossed-posts technique.

Supplies:
- string of beads (about 150g, 6oz of beads for one flower)
- zinc-coated wire, no. 50
- rigid stem, 60cm (2')
- pliers
- wire cutters
- silk thread to match bead color
- craft glue

1 – Cut four pieces of wire. Twist together at one end. Work around and gradually increase the beads between one post and the other until you have achieved the desired width (6cm, 2²/₅"). Cut off the string of beads but not the posts.

2 – For the corolla, create 40 couples of petals made of a small petal in front of a large one. After assembling each couple, wind the wires together. The small petal has a central 2cm (⁴/₅") post with three rows worked onto it. The large petal has a 3cm (1¹/₈") post with three rows worked onto it. Leave 5cm (2") of unstrung wire and twist the two strings of beads together.

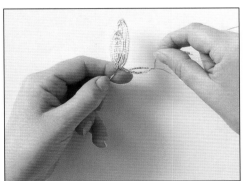

3 – Wind the second string around the post to make the petal.

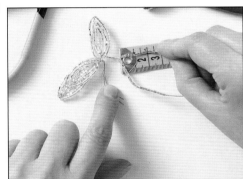

4 – After having made three rows and fastening off the petal's base, bring the wire of the central post full of beads to the petal's base and wind the two unstrung wires for about 0.5cm.

5 – For the large petal, string 3cm (1¹/₈") of beads on one of the two wires to make the post. Work the other wire around it.

6 – After the fifth row, bring the post with the beads to the petal's base and secure it in place.

7 – Every so often, hold the work up in a circle to get an idea of its circumference, since you only need to tighten or to hold the wires more loosely to completely change the corolla's size.

8 – Make the bottom of the flower as you did for the center. Give it a funnel shape, but be careful to wind it on the backside of the sunflower so that it will not be noticeable where the posts have been tied off.

9 – Once you have closed the corolla into a ring, wrap it well with silk thread along its inner border, passing between the petals. Now position the center on the corolla and make new supports.

10 – Position the bottom and, with the pliers, tighten the wires on the upper and lower parts, wrapping them around.

11 – Fasten the four wires well and cut the excess wires. Then, assemble the flower and shape it well.

At this point, attach the rigid stem and, with glue, begin to wrap with the thread. After about 10cm (4"), attach the first of the two leaves you have made with the loop technique. Continue to wrap with the thread and attach the second leaf. Keep threading until you cover the entire stem. Model the petals, and bend the sunflower forward into the classic position.

CORNFLOWER

With the crossed posts-technique, make a dark green funnel-shaped calyx. Cut four pieces of 15cm long wire and wind them together at the base, leaving the last 7cm of the four pieces of wire loose. Tie a string of beads onto the base of the four posts. Begin the first row by stringing three beads; wind the bead string onto the first post. String three beads for the second row, braiding them onto the second post and so on until the fourth row. Wind the rows so the wire is barely visible. Gradually increase the number of beads you string between the posts in each row, so you arrive at eight or ten beads in the last row. The size of the flower depends on the calyx dimensions.

Supplies:
– strings of blue beads for the flower, green for the leaves, and black for the pistils
– zinc-coated wire, no. 40
– rigid stem
– silk thread to match bead color
– craft glue
– pliers
– wire cutters

1 – After making a small loop to secure the beads, string 2cm ($^4/_5$") of beads and, at the top, make the first 2cm ($^4/_5$") loop. Bend it in half and twist it to prevent the beads from falling off.

2 – Make three loops in succession to form four small petals. Wind the loops at the base, string another 2cm ($^4/_5$") of beads and join the two pieces to form the flower. Fill the calyx with lots of flowers. For the flower's center, make six or seven small loops close to each other with black beads. Then, close them in a circle.

3 – Attach the calyx to a rigid stem. Attach the flowers on the inside border of the calyx. Attach the black pistils inside the flowers. Continue filling with flowers so they extend from the calyx for 2cm ($^4/_5$"). With silk thread, attach the lower part of the stems and pistils, which stick out at the calyx's base, and attach the leaves and bud.

SPRINGTIME HARMONY

Arrangements of irises and morning glories, branches of willow and locust. Once the flowers are made with the proper techniques ("post" for the irises and the leaves; "crossed posts" for the morning glories), choose a simple crystal vase and put a number of beads at the bottom of it to add stability and to reflect the light. Begin to position the flowers, starting with the most voluminous. Then, add the leaves and the hanging boughs of morning glories, giving the arrangement a harmonious form.

GAMES OF LIGHT...

The silver and blue of these flowers, made with the post technique, make this a refined arrangement. First, position the heavy flowers, then add the more delicate ones and, finally, add the branches of leaves. Remember to anchor the vase, using beads if the glass is transparent, or sand or rice if it is opaque.

...AND OF COLOR

The multi-colored arrangements of these flowers require the use of all the techniques acquired thus far, including the loop technique for the tight spherical umbrella of the garlic. For the colored flowers it is essential to use real flowers as models to reproduce their details and nuances. At the bottom of the vase you may place a handful of colored marbles that recall the colors of the flower arrangements in order to intensify their visual perception.

SUMMER FANTASY

Poppies, cornflowers, stalks of wheat and lavender, morning glories, majestic sunflowers, and classic summer flowers are gathered masterfully in this luxuriant country bouquet. Place a number of white pebbles on the bottom of the vase, then position the more voluminous sunflowers and the poppies, as the thinner shapes, like the stalks and the morning glories, bending them downward into their typical postures.

Gerberas, irises, narcissuses, made
with the post and loop techniques,
are bound together, with some green
leaves, to brighten their background.
The arrangement is wrapped in a
square of packing paper and tied
with rustic twine of jute, elements
which create a pleasant contrast to
the elegance of the arrangement,
making it all the more contemporary.

RED & GOLD

Sunflowers, tulips, peonies, lilies, stalks of wheat and silver leaves are supported by stems, which in some cases, are reinforced by cords of beads wrapped all around them. Place the flowers in the vase containing beads or pebbles and model them with care. If you create an arrangement to be placed against a wall, make certain that the most important elements are at its center, at a lower level than the others, which radiate outwards, almost as if they were emerging from the wall.

CENTERPIECE

Immaculate lilies, gerberas, and boughs of mimosa make this centerpiece perfect for important occasions and it can be completed by place cards in gold and white beads to give to guests as keepsakes. On a base of small green leaves, construct two bunches of flowers to be placed directly on the table and see to it that the stems at the center of the arrangement overlap. Tie them together tightly with zinc-coated wire and green silk thread. Add the other flowers and leaves in layers to fill in empty spaces. Cover the tied-off center part by wrapping a string of green beads around it. Pass this string delicately among the central leaves and flowers to give the impression of movement to the arrangement. An equally refined alternative is the fuchsia and white arrangement, which enhances the table setting with shades of green.

BOUQUET

Nosegays of violets, dressed in gold, for the classic party favor or place card to give your guests as keepsakes.

A bride's bouquet in pastel colors that will keep forever. Tiny pink roses and yellow and white campanulas are held in a precious doily of beaded lace, made with the loop technique. The stems of the flowers and the components of the doily are tightly tied together at the base with zinc-coated wire and silk thread, then wrapped with a cord of white beads.

Contrasting borders for the two bouquets of gerberas in the silver and blue first version, in yellow and white in the second. They are made in the same way—flowers with the post technique, leaving three of them at the center of the bouquet and placing the others in layers, adding leaves at the borders. Fasten the stems firmly with zinc-coated wire, silk thread, and a little glue. At the end, wrap a cord of silver beads around the first bouquet, a cord of green beads around the second.

A TOUCH OF CLASS

The pure lines of a Medici vase are perfect for this colorful cascade of flowers. Fill the vase with dry floral foam and cover the surface with moss, using glue or a few staples to keep it in place. Begin to insert the flowers, paying attention to the color combinations. Shape the flowers so they hang over the sides of the vase.

On the opposite page
Daisies and cyclamen love knots decorate candles for a romantic dinner. For the knot, make various loops and tie them off at the center with a string of beads; then, attach the fringe, which is made of lengths of strung beads twisted together. Wind zinc-coated wire tightly around the top to fasten it.

TRIMS

1 – To make the cord of the box, measure the lid first with a heavy zinc-coated wire. Then cut the wire, leaving 1cm excess to make sure it fits the box.

2 – Take three strings of beads, tie them firmly to the end of the zinc-coated wire and, holding them flat, wind them in a spiral around the zinc-coated wire.

3 – Twist the beginning and the end of the wires, and position the cord on the box, carefully concealing the tied-off wires under beads. With glue, attach the beads to the velvet, being careful not to stain the box.

4 – Once you have carefully glued the cord around the edges of the lid, position the flower, in this case a golden camellia, and glue it on the side of the box you prefer.

MINIATURE
PLANTS

THE ENCHANTMENT OF SPRING AND THE CHARM OF AUTUMN

Almond

If you want to create a springtime atmosphere or the warm colors of autumn in your home, here is a project that is sure to please. An enchanting composition with delicate almond and peach blossoms, another with maple leaves whose green has turned into the intense orange of fall.

Peach blossoms

Maple

With the following technique you can give form to beautiful fruit trees whose flowers bloom in all their delicate splendor on warm spring days, like the almond with its white petals and the peach with its tender rosy shades. You can also reproduce a symphony of warm autumn colors, which reach their climax in the golden nuances of maple leaves, to create the tree described step-by-step below. The "iron wire" used on the following pages is a colored zinc-coated wire. If no istruction is given, the wire must be no. 40. The wire color, if necessary, is indicated in the supplies list.

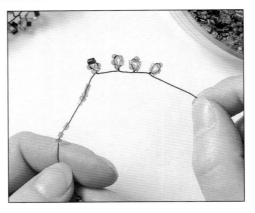

Supplies:
- 100g (4oz) of round beads and bugle beads in yellow, ochre, green, brown, dark beige
- a spool of iron wire, brown or green
- 10 iron stems
- bonsai vase
- moss or pebbles
- rapid drying plaster for planting the tree

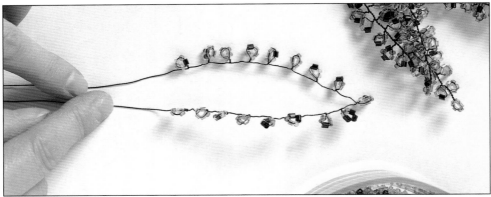

1 – After having strung a number of beads directly onto the spool of wire, leave about 10cm of wire unstrung, then begin to make 17 loops, each having five beads, with 1cm ($^3/_8$") of space between each loop. To make the loop, take five beads in your left hand and, with the help of the right hand, wind the wire around itself until the loop is made.

2 – When you have made all the loops, bend the wire around into a central ring (odd-numbered loop).

3 – Starting from the tip, begin to twist the wire with the loops. In this way, you will have made the leaves.

4 – Using the technique described above, make about 90 small branches of leaves.

5 – To create the trunk, attach the first branch of leaves at the top of a stem. Fasten the second branch at a distance of about 0.5cm ($^3/_{16}$") and repeat the process for 10–15 branches with leaves.

6 – After having attached the leaves, continue to wind the wire around the stem for about 5–6cm (2–2$^2/_5$"). Repeating this process, make about seven or eight small trunks until all the branches of leaves are used.

7 – To assemble, unite the various little trunks, giving them the shape you wish. Should you

wish to make the trunk larger, you may insert several wooden skewers.

Make the little tree, calculating the final height at around 18–20cm (7–8"). Once finished, spread out the ends of the unstrung wire to give them the appearance of roots. This will serve to anchor the plant better in the layer of rapid drying plaster you have already prepared. At this point, plant the maple tree, covering the plaster base with pebbles, or with moss. When all is firmly in place, model the tree.

WISTERIA

Supplies:
- *green beads, beads in various shades of lilac, pink, purple, violet, white, fuchsia*
- *iron wire*
- *iron stems*
- *a root with numerous branches*
- *bonsai vase*
- *moss and pebbles*
- *rapid drying plaster*

Prepare various bead strings on the iron wire leaving 10cm of unstrung wire. Use the loop system to make 60 branches of different lengths.
15 branches: for each branch make 21 loops, each with the following number of beads: 13, 12, 11, 10, 9, 8, 7, 6, 5, 4, 3, 4, 5, 6, 7, 8, 9, 10, 11, 12, 13.
20 branches: for each branch make 25 loops, each with the following number of beads: 15, 14, 13, 12, 11, 10, 9, 8, 7, 6, 5, 4, 3, 4, 5, 6, 7, 8, 9, 10, 11, 12, 13, 14, 15.
15 branches: for each branch make 15 loops, each with the following number of beads: 10, 9, 8, 7, 6, 5, 4, 3, 4, 5, 6, 7, 8, 9, 10.
10 branches: for each branch make 11 loops, each with the following number of beads: 8, 7, 6, 5, 4, 3, 4, 5, 6, 7, 8.
Leave a slight distance between loops.
Starting from the loop with three beads, which makes the branch's tip, twist the loops together.

For the leaves, make 30 or 40 branches from 11 to 13 loops, each with five beads.

1 – Attach the branches of large and small flowers and small leaves onto the tip of a rigid stem to form a cascade of little bunches, winding them uniformly around the iron wire.

2 – Make as many small trunks as there are off-shoots on the root, and try to position them. When you have found the best arrangement, attach all the small trunks together to form the main trunk. At this point, tie the completed plant to the root using the ends of the wire. Prepare the base with plaster and plant the root in it. When everything is firmly set in plaster, cover the base with moss and pebbles. Model the plant.

JASMINE

3 – String four beads, then turn around (stringing respectively three, two, and, at the end, one bead). Leave the two wires hanging without cutting them. Work another four in the same manner.

4 – At this point take two petals, stringing 12 beads onto each of the hanging wires. Begin to construct the calyx. Continue stringing another 12 beads using a leftover wire and a new wire, working around until you have finished all the wires.

5 – When you have filled the four wires with beads, wind them around each other until the beads cannot come off the wires. Prepare about 50 flowers and 10 buds of two different dimensions. These are made with the same technique as used to make the flowers, but by stringing only four petals for the large bud and three for the small bud.

With the loop technique, prepare the neck of the flower. With the green wire and the very light green beads, make a string of about 2.5cm. Bend it in two and make a loop. Without cutting the wire, create another four loops; then, close the wire to form a ring.

For the leaves use the post technique. On a piece of no. 50 zinc-coated wire, string 3cm of beads. Keeping the beads firmly at the center of the post with your left hand, fasten on a string of green beads winding around the center of the post very tightly. Work around the post for five rows and then, with a string of another shade of green, make a contrasting row. Create about 20 leaves, rounded at the top and slightly elongated at the bottom. The leaf must have a right side and a wrong side (on the right side, you must not see the zinc-coated wire, so keep the post under the string of beads when you wind it around.)

To assemble, begin to cover the stem of each individual flower and bud with gutta-percha for 5–6cm (2–2²/₅"). Make many small bunches, tying five flowers and a bud tightly together. On the tip of a rigid stem, 50–60cm (20–24") long, attach a leaf, wrapping it with wire. Then add the first bunch of flowers and a few leaves, continuing to tie them tightly together with iron wire. Continue until completed. Cover the other stem with gutta-percha and twist the branch of flowers to give it a rounded shape. Plant the composition in the plaster and model.

Supplies:
Beads
– 100g (4oz) dark green
– 80g (3.2oz) light green
– 20g (0.8oz) very light green
– 100g (4oz) white with a slightly larger hole
– zinc-coated wire, white, no. 40
– 2 zinc-coated stems
– spool of white wire
– green gutta-percha
– bonsai vase
– rapid drying plaster
– moss or pebbles

1 – Cut about 50cm of white wire and bend it in half. After having strung three beads, bring them to the center; then, cross over the two wires on the two beads, leaving one bead out (passage for the construction of the petal).

2 – String three beads and cross the two wires over each other, threading them through the beads.

FUCHSIA

Supplies:
– fuchsia, silver pink
  (scarab pink), light
  green, and dark
  green beads
– gutta-percha
– iron wire, green
– iron wire, no. 50
– bonsai vase
– rapid drying plaster
– moss or pebbles

Make the calyx with the circle technique (see page 61). String a number of fuchsia beads onto the iron wire and make a first row. On this row, create another two rows in a widening circle. With the same wire, make three more petals just like the first one. For the pistils, string numerous silver pink (scarab pink) beads and form a small ring at the top. Make three or four pistils of different lengths for each flower and wind them together at the base.

With the post technique, use silver pink beads and make about 80–90 petals for the flower's outer part. Make the post with no. 50 iron wire. String 1.5cm of beads onto the post and, with a string of beads of the same color, work two rows using the double point at top and bottom.

1 – Attach the pistils at the center of the calyx, tying them securely with the iron wire.

2 – Under the calyx, insert the five outer petals, shaping them. Cover the base of the flower with 5–6cm (2–2²/₅") of gutta-percha ribbon.

3 – Insert the little leaves (made with the post technique) and wrap them with the gutta-percha.

4 – To prepare the small branches, position the flower at the tip of an iron wire and wrap it with about 3cm (1¹/₈") of gutta-percha. Attach some leaves and wrap it again. Make six or seven branches in this manner. For the large branches, attach several more flowers and leaves.

To assemble, attach a large branch to a new stem and wrap it with the green-colored iron wire. Then, unite some leaves on a new branch, and wrap it with iron wire. Place the branches opposite one another for form and volume. Continue attaching the branches in layers on the trunk and place some leaves at the base to add volume. Once finished, open all the stems at the base to form a pedestal. Position the plant in the center of the vase, and prepare the base of plaster and let it dry well. Place moss or pebbles over the plaster, and model the flowers and leaves.

CHERRY TREE

Supplies:
- *beads in various shades of green*
- *pairs of artificial little cherries*
- *spool of brown wire*
- *flexible and rigid stems*
- *bonsai vase*
- *rapid drying plaster*
- *moss and pebbles*

With the system we will describe for the cherry tree, you can make flowering plants by inserting small, colored flowers among the loops, and you can make trees like the apple, the pear, and the pomegranate by inserting, respectively, small apples, red or green pears, and large crystals in shades of orange.
For all types of plants, first prepare 80 branches of 17 loops made solely with green beads. Then make about 20 branches of 15, 13 and 17 loops, inserting small artificial fruits, which you will find in arts and crafts stores.

1 – Leaving 7cm of wire unstrung, string many green beads on the brown wire. Make a branch of 17 small loops, each with five or six beads about a centimeter from each other. Once again, leave 7cm of wire unstrung.

2 – For the construction of the branches that have fruits, cut about 50–60cm of wire in length. Start stringing six beads and slide them to the middle of the wire. Make the first loop, twist the two wires, then make other loops. To attach the fruits, string three beads on one of the two wires, then a fruit, then another three beads. Close the loop. Continue making the loops necessary for this type of branch, attaching the desired number of fruits.

To assemble, attach the first branch on a flexible stem, beginning at the tip, and wind with about 1cm of iron wire. Attach another branch and continue to wind the wire, attaching also the branches with fruit. On each stem, attach, seven, eight or nine branches, respectively.
Prepare about 10 branches made in this manner and wind the wire around them for about 5–6cm (2–2²/₅"). Cut a rigid stem in half; then, fasten the various completed branches onto the rigid stem with uniform rows of wire, twisting the wire for about 4–5cm (1³/₅–2").

To construct the trunk, cut some rigid stems. Continue to add branches, inserting the stems which have been cut, to add strength. Continue until all the branches have been attached and wrap the wire around the entire length of the trunk.

Model the branches, intertwining them to give the small plant a harmonious and realistic appearance.

Place the plant at the center of the vase and pour the plaster. Let it dry completely and, once you are certain of its stability, cover the base using the moss and pebbles.

PYRACANTHA

Supplies:
- *red and green beads*
- *green and brown iron wire*
- *iron stems*
- *an attractive root*
- *bonsai vase*
- *rapid drying plaster*
- *moss or pebbles*

1 – After having strung several red beads onto the wire (without cutting the wire), leave 10cm of wire unstrung and begin the beadwork. Take five beads from the string and wrap them together to form a small loop. Continue in this way to form six more loops very close together.

2 – After having made the six loops, twist the wires, cutting them off at equal lengths.

3 – Squeeze the loops to give them the form of a little ball. Make about 250 of them; their number may vary according to the dimensions of the root. In the meantime, with the green beads you will have made about 80–90 leaves, each made from eleven loops of five beads. Leave 10cm of unstrung wire at each end. Between one loop and another leave a space of about 1cm ($^{3}/_{8}$").

4 – With the different pieces, make some small branches by alternating leaves and balls in a harmonious way. Attach all the various pieces to the stem, which functions as support, by wrapping it with wire.

Make many branches according to the dimensions of the root and prepare the central branch, which functions as a support, by attaching the balls and the leaves with iron wire. Attach the branches previously constructed adapting them to the shape of the root (every so often place the pieces against the root to give it an ideal shape.)
Once you have finished all components, tie them to the root with the iron wire. Prepare the plaster and insert the plant. Be careful not to dirty the root. When the arrangement is well set, model it and cover the base with moss or pebbles.

LANTANA

Supplies:
- *cobalt blue and green beads*
- *brown iron wire*
- *flexible iron stems*
- *bonsai vase*
- *silicone*
- *moss*

Make 170–180 little green leaves formed by loops, each with seven beads, leaving about 30cm of unstrung wire at the beginning and end. With the strings of cobalt blue beads, make 50 small balls from 11 loops, each with five beads. To make the balls, after you make the 11 loops, wrap them around themselves to form a little ball, leaving 30cm of unstrung wire at beginning and end. When you have completed all of the components, assemble the small branches.

1 – Take a ball and, leaving a space of 2–3cm ($^4/_5$–$1^1/_8$"), attach a little leaf on the wire wrapping the wire for about 2 cm ($^4/_5$").

2 – Continue to wrap more leaves on the base wire. Create about 50 small branches with a ball and leaves according to the following instructions:
– ten branches with ball and seven leaves
– nine branches with ball and six leaves
– nine branches with ball and three leaves
– eight branches with ball and five leaves
– six branches with ball and four leaves
Follow the technique until all the components are used.

3 – Take one or two branches and, holding them together, begin to tie them with the iron wire.

4 – Continue to unite the bunches, giving them an umbrella shape. After attaching the branches, twist together all the hanging wires, giving the trunk the shape you like. At the end, you may divide the wires and twist them to make surface roots. When you have achieved the desired effect, fix the plant firmly to the vase using the silicone. Cover with a thin layer of moss and, if you wish, fill the vase with decorative elements, found in shops that sell dried flowers.

CLASSIC BONSAI

Supplies:
- *100g (4oz) of round and bugle beads (yellow ochre, green, brown, dark beige)*
- *spool of wire, brown*
- *or green*
- *10 iron stems*
- *bonsai vase*
- *rapid drying plaster*
- *moss or pebbles*

Make 240–250 small balls made of eight loops with six beads each.
When you have made the loops, join them to obtain a rounded shape. Leave about 10cm of unstrung wire at the base of every ball and cut the excess wire.

1 – With the help of an iron stem; curl some balls to create volume as you construct the plant.

2 – Using an iron stem, make a branch by placing the first balls at the tip and fasten by wrapping iron wire around them.

3 – Attach 15 balls to make a small branch. Continue to wrap the wire for 5–6cm (2–2²/₅").

Make in this way:
- two branches with 15 balls
- two branches with 25 balls
- two branches with 35 balls
- two branches with 45 balls

After completing all the branches, assemble the bonsai. Begin by uniting the two smallest branches, winding the iron wire around for 2–3cm (⁴/₅–1¹/₈). Position the next two branches (those with 25 balls), attaching them opposite each other. Continue in this manner, first attaching the smallest branches to the largest. Wrap the iron wire around all the components. If you wish to widen the trunk, add some small sticks, covered with the iron wire. The larger the dimension of the trunk, the steadier your composition will be.

Once you finish the plant, place it in the vase and secure it with plaster, being careful not to stain the trunk. When it is well set, arrange the branches so that the bonsai appears as natural as possible.

Supplies
- *100g (4oz) of scarab purple beads and green beads*
- *an attractive root*
- *bonsai vase*
- *spool of zinc-coated wire, brown or green*
- *rigid and flexible stems*
- *rapid drying plaster*
- *moss and pebbles*

1 – String many purple beads onto the wire, leaving about 10cm of unstrung wire. Begin to make some loops, starting with a loop of 11 beads. Leave about 1cm (³/₈") of space between the loops. Proceed making, in this sequence, loops with ten, nine, eight, seven, six, five, four, three beads, then four, five, six, seven, eight, nine, ten, 11 beads.

2 – After having made the loops, twist them together to make a branch. Make about 45–50 branches in this manner.

3 – Make each branch into a bunch of grapes by squeezing all the loops together and giving the branch the shape of a small cone.

4 – With the help of a crochet hook, wrap the unstrung part of the wire into a spiral. Then with the green beads, make 80–85 branches of leaves, each with 11 loops of five beads each. Leave a piece of unstrung wire at the end of each branch to be used during the assembly of the plant.

5 – Position the bunches of grapes and the leaves on the stems, alternating them as you wish to achieve a pleasing effect.

6 – Every so often, place the composition on the root to shape it more harmoniously. Once you have used up all the various components, tie the composition to the root with the iron wire. Add a few branches of leaves to the base of the root, to obtain a more realistic look. Once the composition is assembled, prepare the plaster and anchor the plant, trying not to stain the root.
When the plaster has hardened, cover the base with moss and pebbles and add the finishing touches by seeing to it that all bunches of grapes are hanging downward.

WILLOW

Supplies:
- *green beads with holes of different sizes*
- *wooden board, long and narrow*
- *three spools of brown iron wire*
- *bonsai vase*
- *rapid drying plaster*
- *moss and pebbles*

Start this composition with the trunk.
Wrap the three spools of brown wire around the wooden board, positioned vertically.

1 – When the board has been completely wrapped, cut the wire at both ends with a pair of strong scissors. Secure one end so that it will not prick you while you work, and twist the wires tightly to give shape to the trunk.

2 – Model the plant's branches, dividing the wires and intertwining them as you please.

3 – In order to make the branches you may use two different techniques, using beads with holes of different sizes.
With the first one, you string a bead on one wire, then you wrap another wire around the bead to secure it. Proceed this way until you reach the end of both wires.

4 – With the second method cross the wires inside the bead. Proceed until you arrive at the end of the wires. This procedure is feasible only with beads having slightly larger holes.

5 – Twist the wires themselves and cut the excess wire.

6 – Continue making the branches with the technique you have chosen until you have a sufficient number of branches to create the desired volume and effect.

Anchor the plant with plaster. When the plaster has hardened, cover the surface with moss and pebbles. Model the branches to give the plant its classic shape.

SNOW PLANT

Supplies:
- white beads
- small, star-shaped transparent and white flowers
- zinc-coated white wire
- flexible stems
- bonsai vase
- plaster
- moss

1 – String a bead on a piece of white wire.

2 – Bend the wire in half and insert the two ends into the hole of a flower.

3 – String a white bead on one of the two wires coming out of the flower. Twist the wires at the base of the flower to secure the bead.

4 – Prepare about 100 little flowers, half white and half transparent. Then make 60 all-white branches with seven loops, each loop having seven beads.
Having completed each individual component, start forming different types of bunches:
– bunches made with three or four transparent flowers and five white ones (or vice versa), joined together with one of the wires coming out of the flowers;
– bunches made like the previous ones, but also having five branches of white leaves attached to their base;
– bunches made only of white flowers (six or seven);
– bunches made only of leaves.
The bunches are tied by winding the iron wire uniformly for 3–4cm (1 1/8–1 3/5").

5 – Begin to make the branches of the plant. Attach the first bunch to the tip of a flexible stem. At the end of the part already covered with wire, wind another couple of centimeters of white wire and attach a second bunch.

6 – Attach a new bunch, continuing to wrap with the white wire. Continue this way until you have used all of the bunches.

To assemble, cut a flexible stem in half and attach the individual branches to create the plant's structure. Then, model as you please. To slightly enlarge the trunk you may insert small wooden sticks during the winding process. Once the composition is complete, pour the plaster into the vase and put the plant in it. When the plaster has hardened, cover the surface with moss.

CANDLELIT FIR TREE

Row 4: Three branches of 13 loops with 16 beads each; four branches of 13 loops with 16 beads each (six green loops, candle, seven green loops).
Row 5: Three branches of 15 loops with 16 beads each; four branches of 15 loops with 16 beads each (seven green loops, candle, eight green loops).
Row 6: Four branches of 17 loops with 16 beads each; four branches of 17 loops with 16 beads peach (eight green loops, the candle, nine green loops).
Row 7: Five branches of 19 loops with 16 beads each; five branches of 19 loops with 16 beads each (nine green loops, the candle, 10 green loops).

Assembly:
Row 1: Position the seven-loop branches on four stems, united by wire to make the trunk.
Row 2: Attach the nine-loop branches.
Row 3: Attach the 11-loop branches.
Row 4: Attach the 13-loop branches.
Row 5: Attach the 15-loop branches.
Row 6: Attach the 17-loop branches.
Row 7: Attach the 19-loop branches with candles.
Row 8: Attach the remaining 19-loop branches.
For the rows, attach the branches with candles uniformly.
At the end, spread the four stems and wind them around themselves to form a pedestal.

Supplies:
– dark green, white, red, gold beads
– flexible stems
– zinc-coated wire, green or brown

1 – Cut a piece of wire 50–60cm, slide 16 beads to the center and make a loop. Twist the two wires together for about 1cm. On one of the two wires, insert another 16 beads and make a second loop, twisting together. On the other wire, string five white, three red and another five white beads.

2 – Twist the beads together to form a small candle. You may substitute a gold bead for one of the red ones to make the flame.

3 – Create a third loop next to the candle and finish the branch, leaving 10cm at the beginning and end of the loops and a space of 2.5cm (1") between loops.

Row 1: Three branches of seven loops with 16 beads each.
Row 2: Two branches of nine loops with 16 beads each; four branches of nine loops with 16 beads each (four green loops, candle, five green loops).
Row 3: Four branches of 11 loops with 16 beads each.

SILVER AND GOLD FIRS

Supplies:
- gold beads
- zinc-coated gold wire
- 4 flexible stems
- bonsai vase
- plaster

String many beads on the gold wire, leaving 10cm of unstrung wire at both ends. Make a branch with a single loop of 20 beads for the treetop. Start making the branches as follows:
- three three-loop branches with 13 beads
- three five-loop branches with 13 beads
- four seven-loop branches with 13 beads
- ten nine-loop branches with 13 beads
- ten 11-loop branches with 13 beads
- four 13-loop branches with 13 beads
Leave a space of 2.5cm (1") between each loop to twist and strengthen the branches.

After making all the branches, assemble the tree. Tie together the four flexible stems for the trunk's skeleton.

1 – Attach the branch with 20 beads to the tip of the trunk to form the treetop, and wrap tightly with the gold wire for about 2cm (⁷/₈"). Continue positioning the branches with three loops, wrapping with the wire. On row 2, attach the three branches with five loops, positioning them so that they fill in the empty spaces left by the preceding row.

2 – On row 3, attach the four branches with seven loops positioning them again to fill in the empty spaces.

In row 4 and 5, attach the branches with nine loops. Proceed until you reach the last row with the longest branches.

Continue to wrap the trunk with the gold wire for 4–5cm (1³/₅–2"). Use plaster to anchor the tree in a small pot and arrange the branches.

For a more stylized composition, spread out and cover the stems at the base with gold wire. Twist them into spirals to form a pedestal.

JEWELRY

TOOLS

LOOPED CHOKER

This type of necklace is both easy to make and very striking, suited for all styles of clothing. Once you master the basic technique, you can create a variety of very beautiful pieces.

Supplies:
– hypo-allergenic
  zinc-coated wire
– colored crystals and
  beads
– needle-nosed pliers
– hook and eye clasp
– cord cap
– pliers
– wire cutters

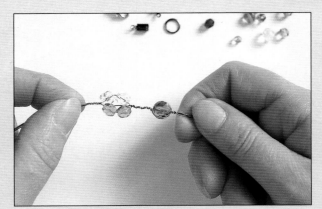

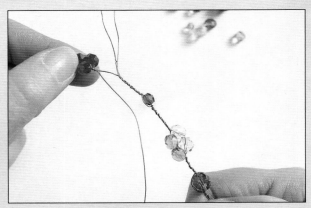

1 – Twist three wires together for about 3cm. String a colored crystal on the central wire.

2 – Bring the two lateral wires down the sides of the crystal, then twist the three wires together for about 2cm. String two crystals on one of the two wires and two other crystals in a contrasting color on the other wire.

3 – Twist the wires together into a 2cm cord.

4 – String a crystal on the center wire and twist the three wires again for about 2cm. On one of the two lateral wires, string three crystals spacing them about 3cm from the point where the wires separate. Go backwards twisting the two wires that hold the three crystals.

5 – Proceed in the same way with the other lateral wire. Using the same technique, continue stringing the beads and crystals until you reach the desired length for the choker.

6 – To attach the clasp, after you twist the wires into a cord for a couple of centimeters, string a cord cap with a hole and, using the pliers, squeeze the clip shut.

7 – After you widen the hole, insert the hook part of the clasp and use pliers to squeeze the hole shut. On the other end, insert a wire-cap with an eye clasp.

SPRING-COIL CHOKER

Supplies:
- spring coils
- hypo-allergenic zinc-coated wire
- coral red beads
- glue for glass
- pliers

With the technique described below, you can make a variety of beautifully coordinated belts and chokers. The first step is to purchase spring coils, which can be found in specialized costume jewelry and crafts stores.

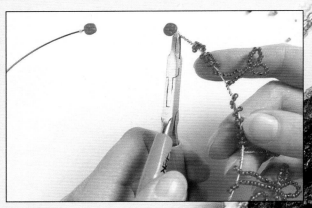

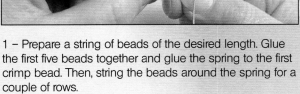

1 – Prepare a string of beads of the desired length. Glue the first five beads together and glue the spring to the first crimp bead. Then, string the beads around the spring for a couple of rows.

2 – With the same string of beads, use the loop technique to build little branches. A couple of centimeters from the spring, make the first loop and twist together at its base to close it. Make another loop, then make a few rows with the string of beads. Make another branch with three loops, twisting the wires at the base. Make a few rows around

and then make another branch of three loops covered to the base with beads.

3 – Proceed with the same system creating a series of branches separated by rows of beads until you reach the end of the spring. A useful tip: As you work, use tongs to hold the beads firmly and to avoid touching the glue with your fingers.

4 – Wind the string of beads carefully around the spring to avoid leaving unattractive empty spaces.

With the same technique you can make a blue choker with crystal pendants alternating with loops of beads as pictured in the illustration. Or use your imagination to create your own combinations! You can also make a simple belt, of the same color of beads, to match the choker.

JEWELRY WITH SPACER BARS

With this technique you can make unique and striking necklaces. The use of spacer bars allows for a harmonious distribution of the beads and the creation of very characteristic pieces, some with many rows of beads and exquisite pendants, closed using beautiful snap-hooks.

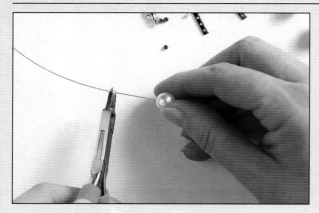

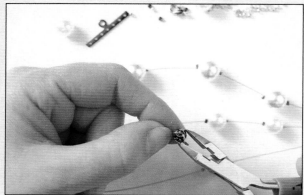

Supplies:
- *covered wire for necklaces*
- *beads and crystals in chosen colors*
- *bugle beads*
- *crimp beads*
- *spacer bar*
- *clasp*
- *cord caps*
- *pliers*

To better illustrate the technique using crimp beads, the following is a classic ivory pearl necklace. With all materials at hand, place a soft cloth on your working table, to keep the pearls from rolling. Cut the wires to the desired length and position them in relation to the project you wish to create. Divide the pearls and crimp beads to have them close at hand.

1 – On the already-cut wire, begin by stringing a crimp bead, then string a pearl, and then another crimp bead at the desired distance.

2 – With the pliers, tighten the crimp bead well to secure the pearl on the wire.

3 – Measure the selected distance again, and string a crimp bead, a pearl and another crimp bead. Continue this way for the length of the necklace.

4 – For necklaces with many strings of beads, it may be necessary to use a spacer bar. This is a little bar with a hook and holes that you choose in relation to the number of strings you wish to make. An alternative is to gather the strings of beads in a cord cap.

5 – To attach the spacer bar, once all the strings of beads are ready, string a crimp bead. Pass each string through a hole and then into the crimp bead, squeezing it well shut.

6 – If the strings of the necklace are heavy, you may wish to use two crimp beads.

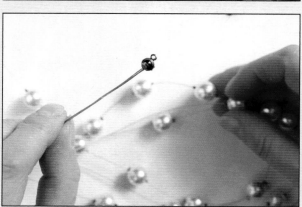

Unique glass bars called bugle beads alternate with red crystals to make this necklace a precious ornament. The various strings are united with a very tight knot and are gathered in cord cap with an eye. A little glue is used in the cord cap, which is then squeezed tightly with pliers.

INTERTWINED JEWELRY

With the intertwining technique you can create particular pieces of jewelry. The bracelet illustrated below, in the step-by-step instructions, if made with beads of high quality and pure colors, can be compared to a piece of jewelry made with real, precious stones. The same is true for the elegant "silver, diamond and hematite" necklace and for the pendant choker in the same colors.

1 – For the bracelet, take a nylon string and bend it in half, making a small loop in the middle, which you will close with a crimp bead using pliers. This fixed loop, easy to hold in your hand, will facilitate the whole working process. At this point, string two beads on one of the strings and one bead on the other string.

2 – Cross one of the two strings through the central crystal and pull the strings firmly as they come out.

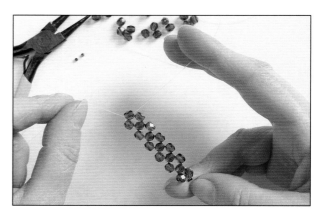

3 – Continue to braid the strings through the central crystal, always stringing two crystals on one string and one crystal on the other.

4 – As you keep working, a basic mesh of little joined flowers will emerge.

5 – To continue to work in length, intertwine the strings, not on the central bead, but on one of the two lateral beads. String two beads on one string.

6 – Make the other string pass through the second bead of the preceding row; then string another bead. In this way you will have started another row.

7 – Continue in the same way with each successive row, always using the upper bead of the preceding row to intertwine.

8 – When the work is finished, fasten the strings well with a crimp bead and squeeze with the pliers.

9 – Passing a piece of string through the beads, make a loop at the beginning and end of the bracelet, which you will close with two crimp beads to use as a clasp.

With the intertwining technique, the more skilled bead workers will be able to make this pretty evening bag.

MORE INTERTWINING

Step-by-step instructions for further intertwining are given on the following pages. Before long, you'll have made exquisite necklaces, a cigarette lighter holder, or a make-up case you can show off on gala nights. At first glance, the different technique may seem long and difficult, but anyone can do it with a little practice.

Supplies:
- zinc-coated iron wire, no. 30
- beads in selected colors
- needle-nosed pliers
- wire cutters

1 – To make this original cigarette lighter holder, intertwine two wires at the base. String two beads on one wire and one bead on the other. Then, pass this last wire through the hole of the second bead of the other wire. In this way a small flower will form. Keep working until you achieve the desired dimension for the base.

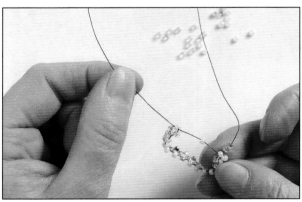

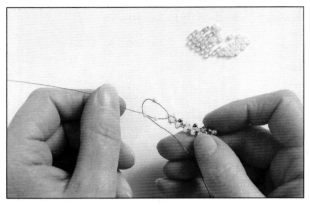

2 – Close the base in a ring, stringing one bead on a wire and passing with this wire through the hole of the initial middle bead. On the other wire, string two beads.

3 – String one bead on the wire coming out of the middle bead and cross over, inserting the wire through the hole of the second of the two beads to form the second row's first flower.

4 – Pass the wire through the base bead and pull it gently.

5 – Then, proceed to form other flowers.

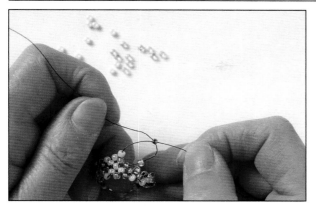

6 – This is how the wire looks that comes out of the base beads. The wire with two beads is intertwined with the wire that holds a single bead.

7 – The illustration shows how the wires look at the completion of the first row.

If, during the work, the wire should break, attach a new wire by passing it gently through some beads and, using pliers, intertwine it with the wires of the beads.

Weave the bottom by passing the wire from one bead to the other, continually filling the wire with beads until all the beads for the base are used up, as if you were sewing. With this system you can also cover boxes, or make book covers, belts and straps for sandals.

Below: A charming red crystal necklace made with the intertwining technique.

BRAID

Supplies:
– light malleable zinc-coated wire, no. 20
– colored beads and crystals
– cord caps
– hook and eye clasps
– pliers
– wire cutters

  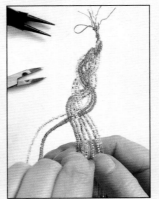 

1 – Cut nine pieces of malleable wire, each 90cm long. String beads onto these wires. To make the necklace more luminous, string crystals among the beads.

2 – Braid the nine strings of beads together; divide them in three groups, each having three strings, alternating the colors as you wish.

3 – Begin to braid, but not too tightly, keeping the necklace flexible.

When you reach the desired length, twist the wires together on both ends and cut off the excess. Cover the remaining stubs of wire with cord caps and attach a hook and eye clasp.

CROCHETING

Supplies:
- *hypo-allergenic wire*
- *crystals of various sizes*
- *a crochet hook, no. 2.5*
- *clasp*
- *rings*
- *pliers*
- *wire cutters*

1 – String the necessary crystals on the wire and, with the beginning part of an unstrung wire, make a base chain (keeping the wire flexible) of equal length to the choker. Work single crochets in each of the chain stitches, stringing crystals whenever you wish. Wrap the wire around the crochet hook, stick it into the chain stitch, catch the wire with the crochet hook and pull it back through the chain stitch. You will now have three loops on the hook; wrap the wire around the hook one more time and pull it through the three loops.

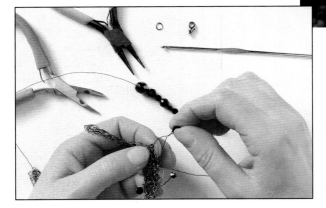

2 – While you crochet the mesh, you can make some pendants with crystals on wire, maintaining a distance equal to the pendant length between the wire and the last completed crochet. Twist the wire together from the base of the crystal to the last crochet completed. Continue crocheting.

3 – To close off the necklace, attach the clasp to the first chain stitch, wrapping it well with the wire left at the beginning. Cut off the excess.

4 – At the other end, slightly open the ring of the clasp to slip over one of the outermost crochets and then close the ring by squeezing tightly with pliers.

SIMPLE NECK WIRE

Supplies:
- scalloped rigid
  neck wire
  hypo-allergenic
- pendant to cover
  with beads
- zinc-coated wire
- beads

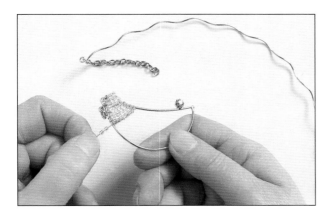

1 – Using the zinc-coated wire, make a string of beads. To cover the skeleton of the pendant, wrap the end of the string of beads firmly around one end of the pendant. Then, gradually fill in the skeleton with the strung beads.

2 – Make tight rows, very close to one another, being careful not to overlap. Next to the pendant you can attach other decorations, like flowers and leaves.

On this refined fishnet choker, you can make flowers or other decorations by passing the wires through the already-prepared fishnet base. Another alternative is to crochet the designs you like on the base, using a string of beads and crystals made with no. 30 zinc-coated wire.

KNITTING
WITH BEADS

And now it's time to use your knitting needles!
You will use them just as you would with yarn,
only your thread is more precious and your
creations release bright splashes of light.

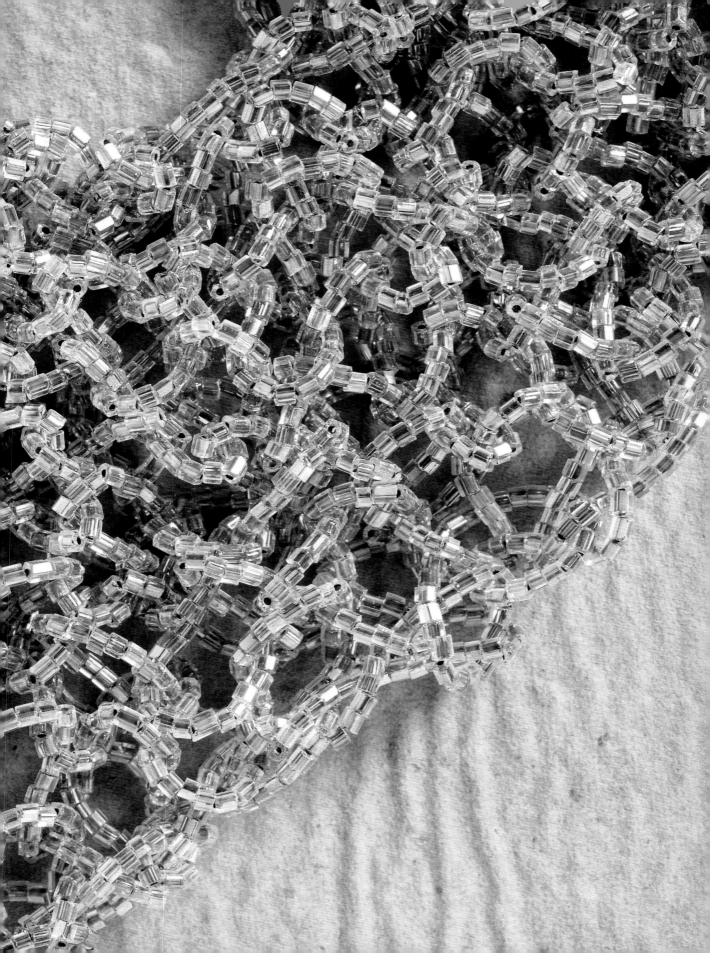

Supplies:
- zinc-coated wire for knitting or crochet
- knitting needles, no. 7
- beads and crystals
- 40cm (16") of rubber tube
- metal hoops
- silk lining material
- wire cutters

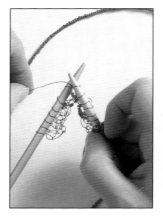 

2 – Begin to knit; put the needle with the cast-on stitches in the left hand, the empty needle and the wire in the right hand. Place the point of the needle into the front of the stitch. Bring the wire under and over the top of the right-hand needle. Draw the wire through the stitch, making a new stitch on the right-hand needle. Continue this process, sliding some beads along the wire as you work it to obtain stitches made only with beads.

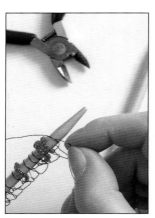 

1 – After stringing a number of beads on the wire, mix them with crystals of the same color, cast on 17 stitches. Begin by making a loop with your right hand. Then, with your left, pass it through the wire, drawing this new loop onto the needle. Repeat 17 times.

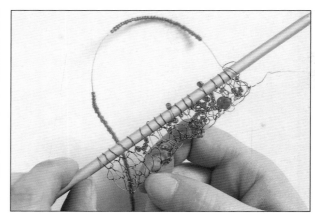

3 – Knit two rectangles of the desired length for the purse (bind off the stitches as you would normally). Make the base of the purse knitting a rectangle of the correct size. Sew the pieces together using the iron wire. For the strap, at the ends of a piece of rubber tube, insert with pressure a hook and eye, which you will sew onto the purse with the iron wire. You may finish off the strap of the purse, using loops of beads, or with a fringed hem at the base made in the same way.

To make this cute little shoulder bag, string 40g (1.6oz) of beads on a cotton thread in a matching beads color.

Knit 14 stitches with no 1.5 needles and work flat, inserting a bead every two stitches. Gradually increase the number of beads, stringing up to 12, always leaving two stitches free. When you reach the desired length, make the back of the purse, progressively decreasing the number of beads.

To make the front flap that closes the purse, continue working with the same number of stitches for a couple of centimeters; then, begin to decrease the stitches laterally until there is only one stitch left on the needle. Continue working another nine stitches and close them off into a loop that serves as a buttonhole.

For the strap, string the number of beads necessary to reach the desired length and attach them at the corners with a hook and eye.

PURSE WITH NEEDLE-STRUNG STRAP

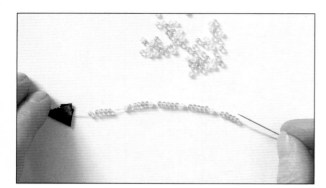

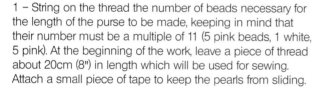

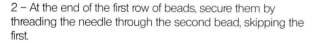

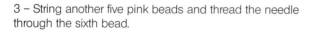

Supplies:
- cotton thread for beads
- colored beads
- beading needle
- adhesive tape

4 – Continue in the same manner, keeping the thread loose, until you reach the desired dimensions. When you have used all the thread, attach the new thread, threading it through a few strung beads. Make a few knots that will be hidden between the beads. Along the seams it is important that the thread comes out on the same side every time.

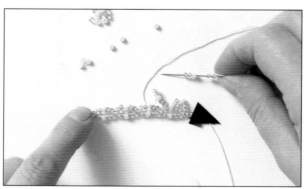

1 – String on the thread the number of beads necessary for the length of the purse to be made, keeping in mind that their number must be a multiple of 11 (5 pink beads, 1 white, 5 pink). At the beginning of the work, leave a piece of thread about 20cm (8") in length which will be used for sewing. Attach a small piece of tape to keep the pearls from sliding.

2 – At the end of the first row of beads, secure them by threading the needle through the second bead, skipping the first.

3 – String another five pink beads and thread the needle through the sixth bead.

To make the thin shoulder strap, string
a number of beads on a nylon thread of
the desired length. After making some
knots at the ends, secure them by lightly
burning the stub of thread. Finish by
sewing onto the shoulder strap.

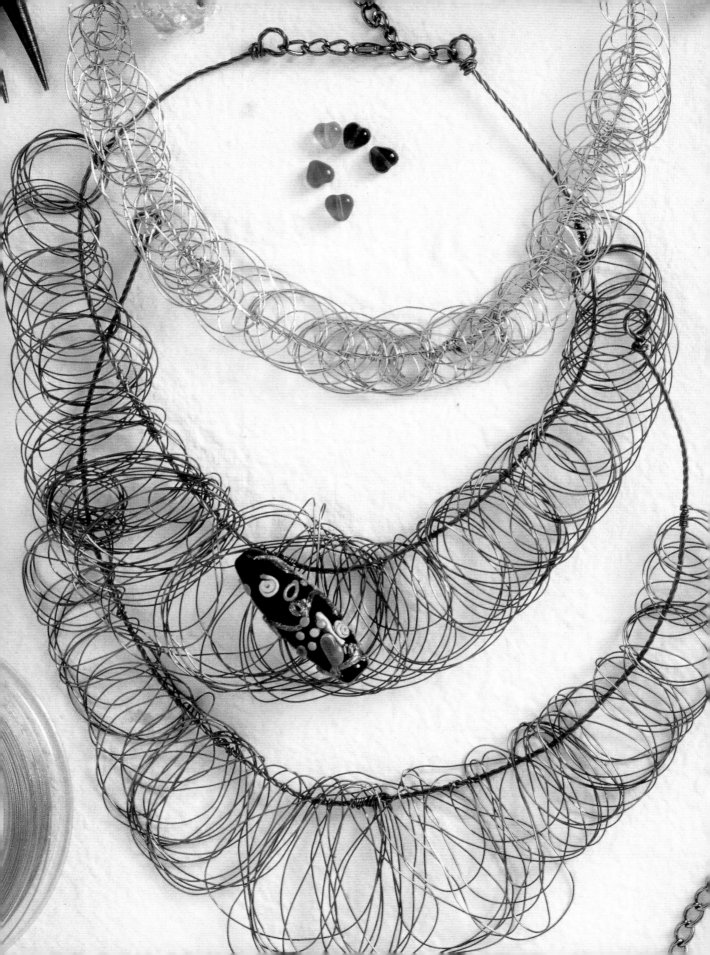

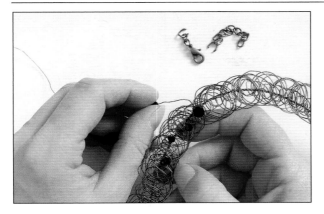

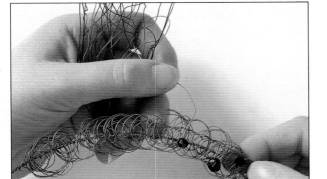

SPIRALED CHOKER

Supplies:
- twisted wire stem
- crystals
- hypo-allergenic, zinc-coated wire
- clasp
- chain
- pliers

1 – First cut many pieces of wire about 1m in length. Wind the wire, squeezing tightly one end, at about 5cm (2") distance from the beginning of the twisted stem. Then start winding the wire in a spiral, forming rings. Intertwine the wire around the rings, creating rounded, loose spirals, continuing to string the wire into spirals to interconnect them.

2 – When the first piece of wire is finished, wrap it around the stem to attach it. Take another end, attach it to the stem, string a few crystals and continue creating spirals, both with and without crystals, alternating larger and smaller spirals. Overlap the various rings to obtain a dense thread.

3 – Proceed until you reach the end of the stem, stopping at about 5cm from the end and fastening the wire well. Thickness, width and volume are given by the various rows and intertwining. When completed, it is possible to shape the spirals by squeezing them between your hands.

4 – With pliers, make a ring by winding the stem around in a circle. Open up the ring of the clasp enough to insert the ring of wire into it, and then close it up.

5 – On the opposite side, make a ring. Insert a clasp onto the ring. If you wish to lengthen the choker, attach a piece of chain to the ring.

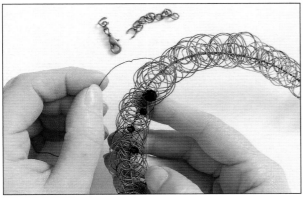

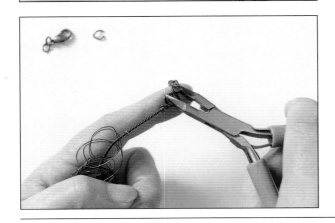

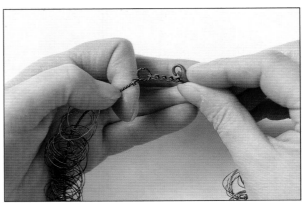

RINGS

Supplies:
- black and ruby colored crystals
- zinc-coated wire, no. 50
- needle-nosed pliers
- wire cutters

Rings have always been objects of great interest. Current fashion trends include showy rings and these, made with colorful crystals and beads, can be mixed and matched for any occasion.

1 – Wind the no. 50 wire a couple of times around your ring finger and, once you have the correct size, squeeze the wire together with the pliers.

2 – On the unused wire, string a black crystal, a burgundy and again a black one; then wind them around the ring of wire, keeping the stones on the upper part.

3 – String new stones as you wish and intertwine them with the others, keeping the wire loose.

4 – Continue to add new stones of different sizes with the same technique, shaping the ring. Every so often, try on the ring to see how it looks.

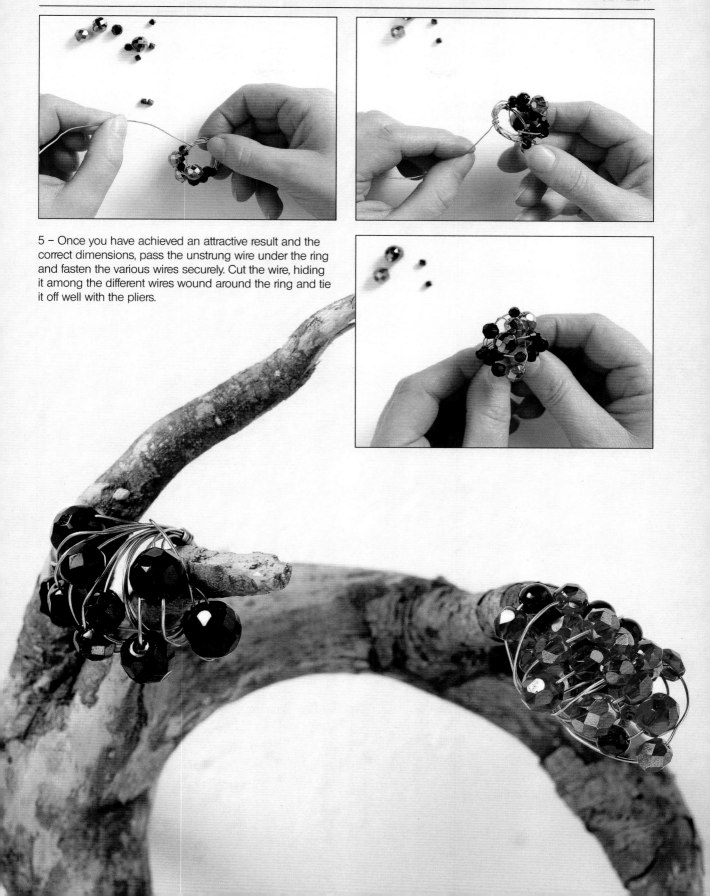

5 – Once you have achieved an attractive result and the correct dimensions, pass the unstrung wire under the ring and fasten the various wires securely. Cut the wire, hiding it among the different wires wound around the ring and tie it off well with the pliers.

GLOSSARY

Anima – Center of the bead, a base in opaque glass.

Asse – Special cotton thread used to thread beads.

Aventurine – Type of glass obtained in the seventeenth century by a suspension of copper crystals in fused vitreous mass.

Bronzino – Little die in bronze or iron to transform the fused paste into glass cylinders.

Cameo working – Technique for incising glass, applied to objects formed by layers of glass in various colors, in which the outer layer is cut and the layer beneath emerges as background.

Conterie or Seed beads – Type of bead obtained by cutting thin glass rods with holes into small pieces, then rounding them with fusion.

Enamel – Opaque colored glass.

Filigree beads – Beads obtained by artistically working opaque or colored cylinders that are braided, folded or straight.

Flowered beads – Type of oil-lamp beads that are decorated with aventurine and small flowers.

Ice beads – Beads from the Renaissance period obtained through a process that gave them a cracked and opaque appearance.

Impiraresse – Name for women who in the past strung pearls for a living.

Gutta-percha (natural latex) – A tough plastic substance from the latex of several Malaysian trees of the sapodilla family that resembles rubber but contains more resin and is used especially as insulation.

Jais – Pieces of glass rods with holes that are not rounded.

Mac – Black multi-faceted beads.

Margarite – Small beads cut from thin glass cylinders.

Margariteri – Workers who make the rounded "margarite" beads.

Mariegola – Fraternity of Venetian glassworkers who were governed by a precise set of rules.

Milk-glass or Opaline – Type of opaque white glass obtained in the past by adding to the fused vitreous mass a mixture of lead and tin, or lead and arsenic, or a powder of limed bone. All elements today substituted by fluosilicate or cryolite.

Millefiori mosaics – Glass mosaics obtained by arranging segments of multi-colored glass rods to form a design. Heated in a furnace, they soften and blend with the mass of fused transparent glass, a process that allows the colors to come through.

Mosaic beads – See Millefiori.

Murrine – Pieces of thin glass rods in mosaic colors; or a surface of glass obtained by uniting small, heated glass rods to form a mosaic.

Oil-lamp beads – Beads obtained by the fusion of one or more glass cylinders over the flame of an oil lamp.

Paternosteri – Artisans who produced beads for rosaries.

Paternosters of glass – Probably the name for the first Venetian glass beads that imitated crystal rosary beads.

Perlere or Perleri – Ancient name of oil-lamp beadmakers.

Plume or Swag beads – Obtained by using metal points to give movement to the design of the vitreous paste. Different colors are applied, while still hot, to the beads.

Rosetta beads – Beads obtained by cutting a multi-colored mosaic cylinder, perforating it and grounding it into a round shape.

Schiette beads – Single-colored beads.

Submerged beads – Beads obtained by the hot-working of multi-layer, polychromatic glass.

Submerged glass – Cylinder of glass formed by an inner part and an outer transparent layer (See Millefiori mosaics).

Vette – Very thin threads (flat or round) of glass pulled by hand and used to decorate flowered beads.

Beadwork Supplies

General Supplies

Michaels Arts & Crafts
8000 Bent Branch Drive
Irving, TX 75063
Tel: (214) 409-1300
Web site: http://www.michaels.com

Mail-order art supply:

Dick Blick Art Materials
P.O. Box 1267
695 US Highway 150 East
Galesburg, IL 61402-1267
Toll-free Tel: 1-800-828-4548
Toll-free Fax: 1-800-621-8293
Web site: http://www.dickblick.com

Metalliferous
34 West 46th Street, 2nd Floor
New York, NY 10036
Tel: (212) 944-0909
Toll-free Tel: 888-944-0909
Fax: (212) 944-0644
Web site: http://www.metalliferous.com
Tools & Supplies Questions:
comments@metalliferous.com
A full-service, fully-stocked supplier of
metal, tools, and supplies to
jewelers, crafters, metalworkers, etc.
Good to browse for wire, cord,
thread, needles, crystals, semi-
precious stone and plastic beads

Beads

Beads by Mail
P.O. Box 227
Pembroke, MA 02359
Tel: 781-293-4475
Toll-free order: 1-800-572-7920
Fax: 781-293-6083
Web site: http://beadsbymail.com
Transparent Glass Beads from Czech
Republic, Austria, Germany

Hot Glass Beads
4521 PGA Blvd. #131
Palm Beach Gardens, FL 33418-3997
Tel: 561-371-9021
Toll-free order: 1-888-404-9021
Web site: http://www.hotglassbeads.com

**Via Murano: Venetian Glass Beads
and More...**
c/o Pamela Israel
PO Box 10081
Newport Beach, CA 92658
Tel: 949-706-2898
Fax: 949-706-2895
E-mail: pam@viamurano.com
Web site: http://www.viamurano.com/
Venetian glass beads and sterling
silver findings. Genuine Venetian glass
beads, imported directly from Venice,
Italy, sold at both wholesale and retail

Swest Inc.
11090 N. Stemmons Freeway
PO Box 59389
Dallas, TX 75229-1389
Toll-free Order: 1-800-527-5057
Toll-free Fax: 1-800-441-5162
E-mail: email@swestinc.com
Czech glass beads, precious stone
beads, metal beads, base metal,
beading supplies, tools & kits, findings,
precious metals & wire